THIRD EDITION

Money Matters

Personal and Family Financial Management Simulation

DEAN CLAYTON • LARRY D. COLEMAN

Glencoe
McGraw-Hill

AUTHORS

Dean Clayton (Ed.D.) is professor emeritus, University of Arkansas and former head of the Department of Vocational Education, professor of business education, and a former professor at Northeastern State University in Tahlequah, Oklahoma. He has also held several teaching and administrative positions in schools in Oklahoma and Arkansas.

Larry D. Coleman (Ed.D. and CLU) is emeritus chairperson, professor, Department of Insurance and Risk Management, School of Business at Indiana State University. He has also held teaching and administrative positions at the University of Central Arkansas. Dr. Coleman has served as a consultant and lecturer for numerous universities, businesses, and government agencies.

Send all inquiries to:
Glencoe/McGraw-Hill
8787 Orion Place
Columbus, OH 43240-4027

ISBN: 0-07-823775-0

Printed in the United States of America.

9 10 11 12 13 14 REL 14 13 12 11 10 09

Table of Contents

The *Single* Person

After completing this unit,
you will be able to:

- Prepare a personal balance sheet.

- Prepare a budget.

- Manage a checking account.

- Use a cash record sheet.

- Use a financial record sheet.

- Prepare a budget comparison sheet.

Jerome Roberts graduated from North Carmel High School and in a few months he will be an independent man: he is going to college. His mother impressed upon him the importance of education, which was great except Jerome did not have any idea what he wanted to do with his life. He had thought about becoming a photojournalist since he liked taking pictures for his high school newspaper. He also liked spending his spare time in his room working on his computer. His mother told him to study something he liked doing; college was about studying anything he wanted but it was also preparing him for a career.

After much deliberation, Jerome decided to attend California Community College since they had a reputable computer programming associate degree. After he finished his two-year degree, he would consider pursuing his bachelor of science at a four-year university. For now, he and his mother were satisfied with his decision to attend the community college.

During Jerome's junior year in high school, he started working after school as a salesperson for Millennium Electronics in the camera department. He really liked his job and did not want to quit, but he had to leave for college in the fall, which was 50 miles away from home. Jerome's boss, who supported his continuing his education, arranged for Jerome to transfer to the store closest to his college.

In the middle of the summer Jerome traveled to the college campus for student orientation. One of his challenges was to find a roommate and rent a two-bedroom apartment on campus. He thought about this as he walked with other students on the campus tour. In the student center he saw a pamphlet for the photography club. Immediately he was excited to join this club since he was so passionate about photography. He imagined his degree in computer programming would give him an opportunity to specialize in digital imaging. The opportunities at college seemed limitless to him. He was thrilled to be attending college in a matter of weeks.

Jerome's First Financial Lesson

PERSONAL BALANCE SHEET

This would be Jerome's first time living on his own. His mother helped him prepare a personal balance sheet and budget in order to stay financially organized and responsible. A **personal balance sheet** shows what you own, what you owe, and the difference between these two amounts. **Assets** are what you own. For example, the cash you have in your pocket, the money in your bank account, and your car are all assets.

Table 1.1

**JEROME ROBERTS
PERSONAL BALANCE SHEET**
AUGUST 31, 20--

ASSETS		
Cash	$ 330	
Savings	4,500	
Car	3,200	
Computer	1,200	
Other Assets	800	
Total Assets		$10,030
LIABILITIES		
Computer Loan	$ 530	
Total Liabilities		$ 530
NET WORTH		9,500
Total Liabilities and Net Worth		$10,030

Use the formula to find Jerome's assets. Show your work.
Answer: $530 + $9,500 = $10,030.

Liabilities are what you owe. If you have a balance on a credit card or a car loan, these are liabilities. The difference between your total assets and your total liabilities is your **net worth**. You

Keywords

personal balance sheet – shows what you own, what you owe, and the difference between these two amounts.
asset – an item that a person owns.
liability – an amount that a person owes.
net worth – assets minus liabilities; the difference between what you own and what you owe.

can express this in an equation:

assets − liabilities = net worth.

When you prepare a personal balance sheet list all your assets and add the amounts to get a total. Next, list all your liabilities and add the amounts to get a total.

You can also show the relationship among assets, liabilities, and net worth by changing the formula to: liabilities + net worth = assets; see Table 1.1. Suppose you have $150 in your pocket, $1,200 in the bank, and a car that cost $12,500. Your total assets are $13,850. If your credit card balance is $546 and you owe $5,200 on your car, your total liabilities are $5,746. Your net worth would be $8,104 ($13,850 − $5,746).

MONTHLY BUDGET

A **budget** is a plan that shows your expected income, expenses, and savings for a period of time. You can prepare a budget for any particular period, but most people start with a monthly budget.

Jerome makes $12.50 an hour at Millennium Electronics and expects to work 30 hours a week. Working 30 hours a week equals around 120 hours a month. If you multiply the number of hours per month Jerome works by his hourly rate of pay the result is Jerome's **gross earnings** for the month (120 x $12.50 = $1,500). Although his **income** for the month is $1,500 that does not mean he receives the full amount. There are other factors to be considered.

Employers are required to deduct federal income tax from each employee's gross earnings. State income tax is deducted in most states. The amount of tax that is withheld from an employee depends on several factors including the employee's marital status and how much money the employee earns. Employers also must deduct Social Security and health care taxes from each employee. All of these deductions subtract money from his pay; therefore, Jerome actually takes home about $1,100 each month.

On Jerome's campus tour he met a fellow student, Josh Adams. They were both looking for a roommate, so they decided to live together. They rent a small, two-bedroom apartment and each pays $350 a month. Rent is a **fixed expense** since it requires a payment on a specific date and in a specific amount. There are some fixed expenses, such as insurance and real estate taxes, which are paid

only once or twice a year. When you budget for these expenses, set aside some money each budget period. Divide the total expense by the number of budget periods to find the amount that must be set aside. For example, if your car insurance were $420 every six months, you would budget $70 each month for car insurance ($420 ÷ 6 = $70).

Other expenses the two have to split include the electric and phone bills. Then Jerome also has to budget for **variable expenses** like food and entertainment. He also tries to save $100 every

Table 1.2		

**JEROME ROBERTS
MONTHLY BUDGET**
PREPARED AUGUST 31, 20--

INCOME		
Take Home Pay		$1,100
EXPENSES		
Rent	$350	
Food	200	
Entertainment	100	
Clothing	75	
Car Insurance	60	
Electric	50	
Gas	50	
Computer Loan	50	
Telephone	25	
Miscellaneous	40	
Total Expenses		1,000
Balance Available for Savings		$ 100

Can you name a miscellaneous expense?
Answer: Answers will vary

month and have at least $75 to spend on clothes. Savings is also included as part of a budget. **Savings** is money set aside for emergencies and specific goals. This money should be placed in an account that earns interest and can be withdrawn at any time. After you establish your emergency fund, you can start saving for other financial goals. Jerome's monthly budget for August is shown in Table 1.2.

Jerome's First Month at College

At the new Millennium Electronics location, Jerome is still paid bi-weekly. On payday Fridays, he leaves work a little before five o'clock in order to get to the bank to deposit his $560 paycheck.

On one particular Friday he also deposits $200 from graduation money received from friends and relatives over the summer. Jerome's deposit slip is shown in Figure 1.1.

His rigorous course schedule and part-time job keep him extremely busy. One night as Jerome and Josh were relaxing after dinner watching a baseball game on television, Jerome looked at his watch and realized it was September 1—rent day. That night Jerome wrote a check for his share of the September rent (Figure 1.2).

Normally Jerome saves money by eating lunch at his apartment instead of eating out, but on Tuesdays he doesn't have time to go home since he has to be at work at 12:30 in the afternoon. Instead he withdraws cash from the ATM (Figure 1.3), buys lunch, and studies while he eats a deli sandwich and chips.

By the end of September, Jerome had lived independently for one full month. His mother usually called him on Sunday nights. This Sunday she reminded him to set aside time and look over his **check register** (see Table 1.3) and **bank statement** (see Table 1.4) for the month.

Jerome's balance, according to his check register, is $393.83. The ending balance on his bank statement is $566.08. The bank often provides a **reconciliation form** on the back of the statement (Table 1.5).

After reconciling his bank statement, Jerome deducts $3.75 from his check register balance for the ATM fees.

JEROME'S CASH RECORD SHEET

On the first of September, Jerome had $95 in his pocket. The $95 is his beginning cash balance for September. Each time Jerome withdraws money from the ATM, he enters the amount in the "cash withdrawals column" of the **cash record sheet** (see Table 1.6). This way he can track his out-of-pocket spending. When he spends money he keeps track of the amount that he spends by entering that amount in the proper category column of his cash record sheet. At the end of the month Jerome totals all category columns.

On the last day of September, Jerome has $11 in his pocket. If he takes his beginning cash

Figure 1.1

			DOLLARS	CENTS
Jerome Roberts 2461 Loxley Avenue Carmel, CA 95861	3-94 812	CASH	200	00
		COINS		
Date _____ 9-1 _____ 20 --		CHECKS—List Singly		
		1 13-42	560	00
		2		
		3		
DEPOSIT SLIP		4		
		5		
FIRST NATIONAL BANK OF CARMEL CARMEL, CA 95286		6		
		Sub Total	760	00
		Less Cash Received		
⑆1250063751⑆ 266442		**TOTAL**	760	00

Figure 1.1. Could Jerome deposit his check and cash in an ATM? Answer: Yes.

Figure 1.2

Jerome Roberts
2461 Loxley Avenue
Carmel, CA 95861
No. 101
3-94
812
_____ 9-1 _____ 20--
PAY TO THE ORDER OF _Josh Adams_ $ 350.00
Three hundred fifty and no/100 DOLLARS
FOR USE IN CLASSROOM ONLY
FIRST NATIONAL BANK OF CARMEL
CARMEL, CA 95286
MEMO _Rent for September_ _Jerome Roberts_
⑆1250063751⑆ 266442 ⑈ 101

Figure 1.2. Did Jerome turn in his rent on time or late? Answer: On time.

Figure 1.3

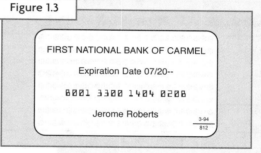

FIRST NATIONAL BANK OF CARMEL
Expiration Date 07/20--
6001 3300 1404 0208
Jerome Roberts
3-94
812

Figure 1.3. What other functions besides withdrawing cash can you use an ATM for? Answer: Deposit, inquiring about checking and savings balances, and (some ATMs) allow you to buy postal stamps.

Keywords

budget – plan that shows your expected income, expenses, and savings for a period of time.

gross earnings – earnings without any deductions.

income – earnings for a certain period.

fixed expenses – expenses that must be paid on specific dates and in specific amounts.

variable expenses – expenses that occur at different times and in different amounts.

savings – money set aside for emergencies and specific goals.

check register – a form or booklet usually found in a checkbook that is used to list all checks, deposits, and ATM transactions.

bank statement – A form sent out by the bank listing all charges and deposits made against a checking account.

reconciliation form – the process of checking a bank statement against the check register.

cash record sheet – a form used to account for your out-of-pocket spending for a specific period of time.

Table 1.3

JEROME ROBERTS' CHECK REGISTER

Check No.	Date	Checks Issued To or Description of Deposit	Payments	✓	Deposit	Balance
	9-1	Deposit–Cash and Paycheck			760.00	760.00
101	9-1	Josh Adams	350.00			410.00
	9-6	ATM Withdrawal	100.00			310.00
102	9-8	Gap	38.40			271.60
	9-14	ATM Withdrawal	50.00			221.60
	9-15	Deposit–Paycheck			558.23	779.83
	9-17	ATM Withdrawal	50.00			729.83
103	9-21	State Farm Insurance Company	60.00			669.83
104	9-26	Josh Adams	44.00			625.83
	9-28	Transfer to Account 213.21	100.00			525.83
105	9-28	Josh Adams	32.00			493.83
106	9-30	Computer City	50.00			443.83
	9-30	ATM Withdrawal	100.00			343.83
	9-30	Deposit–Birthday Gift			50.00	393.83

How many ATM withdrawals did Jerome have from September 1 through September 30?

Answer: Four.

Table 1.4

JEROME ROBERTS' BANK STATEMENT

First National Bank of Carmel Carmel, CA 95286		Jerome Roberts 2461 Loxley Avenue Carmel, CA 95861	

Date: October 7, 20--   Account No. 266442

Beginning Balance	Total Payments	Total Deposits	Ending Balance
-0-	752.15	1,318.23	566.08

Date	Check. No.	Amount Paid	Amount Deposited	Balance
9-1			760.00	760.00
9-7	ATM	100.00		
	fee	1.25		658.75
9-7	101	350.00		308.75
9-8	102	38.40		270.35
9-15	ATM	50.00		
	fee	1.25		219.10
9-16			558.23	777.33
9-18	ATM	50.00		
	Fee	1.25		726.08
9-26	103	60.00		666.08
9-29	Tfer	100.00		566.08

Jerome receives this bank statement in what month?

Answer: October.

in his pocket on September 30. See Jerome's complete cash record sheet.

JEROME'S FINANCIAL RECORD SHEET

Jerome's **financial record sheet** is easy to prepare because he reconciled his bank statement and kept an accurate cash record sheet. Information for the entries comes from his check register, his cash record sheet, and other documents such as sales receipts and bills. The purpose of the financial record sheet is to keep track of how much money he is spending in each category. After completing his financial record sheet he can compare it to his monthly budget.

The first step in preparing a financial record sheet is to transfer all deposits, ATM withdrawals, and payments from his check register to the financial record sheet. Then transfer the balance totals from each category on the cash record sheet to the financial record sheet. Now, add all the columns on the financial record sheet. Table 1.7 shows Jerome's financial record sheet for the month of September.

balance of $95, adds his total ATM withdrawals ($300) and subtracts his total payments ($384) he will get $11. This agrees with the actual cash

Table 1.5

BANK RECONCILIATION FORM FOR JEROME ROBERTS

Bank Statement Balance			$ 566.08
ADD:			
Deposits in Transit			$ 50.00
Total			$ 616.08
SUBTRACT:			
Outstanding Checks			
And Other	104	$ 44.00	
Deductions	105	32.00	
	106	50.00	
	ATM	100.00	226.00
Adjusted Bank Balance			$ 390.08
Checkbook Balance			$ 393.83
Add Interest			
Total			$ 393.83
Deduct Bank Fees			3.75
Adjusted Checkbook Balance			$ 390.08

How could Jerome avoid ATM fees?
Answer: He could withdraw cash from only his banks' ATM locations.

Jerome's Budget Comparison Sheet. After Jerome totals his financial record sheet he is ready to complete the **budget comparison sheet**. A budget comparison sheet lists his budget's estimated expenses, actual expenses, and the difference between those amounts. The budget comparison sheet also lists his estimated income and savings, actual income and savings, and the difference between those amounts. The difference between estimated amounts and actual amounts is called a **variance**.

Keywords

financial record sheet – a form used to account for all receipts of money and payments of money for a specific period of time.
budget comparison sheet – lists budgeted income and expenses, actual income and expenses, and the difference between the two.
variance – when an actual expense or income item is different than an estimated expense or income item.

Table 1.6

JEROME ROBERTS' CASH RECORD SHEET, September, 20--

Date	Description	Cash Withdrawals	Payments	Clothing	Entertain.	Food	Housing	Transportation	Miscellaneous
9-1	Beginning Cash Balance $95								
9-6	ATM	100.00							
9-7	Groceries		55.00			55.00			
	Cleaning Supplies		20.00						20.00
9-9	Movie		12.00		12.00				
9-11	Groceries		32.00			32.00			
9-14	ATM	50.00							
	Gas		15.00					15.00	
9-16	Haircut		25.00						25.00
	Food		14.00			14.00			
9-17	ATM	50.00							
	Groceries		23.00			23.00			
9-19	Concert		30.00		30.00				
9-21	Miniature Golf		8.00		8.00				
	Food		10.00			10.00			
9-25	Groceries		28.00			28.00			
	Gas		12.00					12.00	
9-26	School Supplies		18.00						18.00
	Pizza		15.00			15.00			
9-30	ATM	100.00							
	Movie		12.00		12.00				
	Groceries		55.00			55.00			
	Totals	300.00	384.00	-0-	62.00	232.00	-0-	27.00	63.00
9-30	Ending Cash Balance $11								

How much did Jerome spend on entertainment in September?
Answer: $62.

Table 1.7

JEROME ROBERTS' FINANCIAL RECORD SHEET, September, 20--

Date	Chk.	Description	Receipts	With-drawals	Payments	Clothing	Enter-tainment	Food	Health Care	Housing	Trans-portation	Miscel-laneous	Savings/Investments
9-1		Cash Balance $95											
		Gift	200.00										
		Paycheck	560.00										
	101	Rent			350.00					350.00			
9-6		ATM		100.00									
9-8	102	T-shirts			38.40	38.40							
9-14		ATM		50.00									
9-15		Paycheck	558.23										
9-17		ATM		50.00									
9-21	103	Car Insurance			60.00						60.00		
9-26	104	Electric			44.00					44.00			
9-28		Savings			100.00								100.00
9-28	105	Phone			32.00					32.00			
9-30	106	Computer Loan			50.00							50.00	
		ATM		100.00									
		Birthday Gift	50.00										
		ATM fees			3.75							3.75	
		From Cash Record Sheet			384.00		62.00	232.00			27.00	63.00	
		Totals	1,368.23	300.00	1,062.15	38.40	62.00	232.00	-0-	426.00	87.00	116.75	100.00

Is a financial record sheet accurate without ATM withdrawals?

Answer: No—you must transfer all your deposits, ATM withdrawals, and payments from a check register to financial record sheet.

Table 1.8

JEROME ROBERTS' BUDGET COMPARISON SHEET
SEPTEMBER 20--

Category	Estimated	Actual	Variance
INCOME:			
Salary	$1,000.00	$1,368.23	$ +368.23
EXPENSES:			
Rent	$350.00	$350.00	$ 0
Food	200.00	232.00	+ 32.00
Entertainment	100.00	62.00	- 38.00
Clothing	75.00	38.40	- 36.60
Car Insurance	60.00	60.00	0
Electric	50.00	44.00	- 6.00
Gas	50.00	27.00	- 23.00
Computer Loan	50.00	50.00	0
Telephone	25.00	32.00	+ 7.00
Miscellaneous	40.00	116.75	+ 76.75
Totals	$1,000.00	$1,012.15	+$12.15

What expense categories did Jerome spend more than he estimated?

Answer: Food, telephone, and miscellaneous.

When an actual expense is less than the budgeted expense you have a favorable variance. When an actual expense is more than the budgeted expense you have an unfavorable variance. When actual income is less than budgeted income you have an unfavorable variance, but when actual income is more than budgeted income you have a favorable variance. If Jerome actually saves more than he plans to save then he has a favorable variance. However, if he saves less than he plans then he has an unfavorable variance.

Most budget variances occur when unexpected expenses arise. Table 1.8 shows Jerome's budget comparison sheet for September.

Student *Activities*

This section is designed for you to practice the concepts introduced through Jerome Roberts' experiences in unit one. In these activities, refer back in this unit if you need help with preparation of statements or banking and recordkeeping activities. Additionally, these activities may be completed by numerous methods: manually or automatically (e.g., Microsoft(MS) Money, Quicken, and Excel). Each activity includes software directions if you would like to complete an activity using one of those programs.

———Activity 1———

Maia Lazarus graduated from college two years ago. She is a physical therapist at Buffalo Rehab and specializes in sports injuries. Maia's monthly take-home pay is $3,280 and her current checking account balance as of November 30 is $1,542.36. Maia has her bank transfer $300 from her checking account to her savings account on the first day of each month. The current balance of her savings account is $5,300.

Maia's employer pays for her medical, dental, and life insurance. Her life insurance does not continue if she changes employers, but she can keep the medical and dental insurance for up to two years by paying the insurance premiums. She also has a $50,000 life insurance policy that costs $28 each month. This policy does not have a cash value, which means it is not an asset.

Maia leases a one-bedroom condo for $750 a month. Her furniture has a value of $5,000 and is paid for. She bought a computer for $1,700 and a stereo for $900 on credit last month. Her $2,600 loan is with Electronics Finance Company and the first payment of $108 is due on December 18. Maia also owes $10,500 on her student loan with a payment of $225 on the 15th of each month. Her truck has a value of $8,800. She paid off her car loan several months ago.

REQUIRED: Prepare a personal balance sheet for Maia Lazarus as of November 30 using FORM 1, page 57. You will notice that FORMS (except banking documents) are provided in sequential order beginning on page 55.

In working with an activity, file all FORMS in an IN FILE or an OUT FILE, according to the destination of the document. Thus, the personal balance sheet for Maia is filed in the IN FILE. (You need to provide two folders—one labeled IN FILE and the other labeled OUT FILE.)

Software Directions

How to prepare a personal balance sheet in Microsoft Money:
1. At the top of the screen, click **Accounts**.
2. On the left-hand side of the screen, click **Set up accounts**.
3. Click **Add a new account**.
4. In the associated text box, enter **where the account is held.**
5. Determine if the institution is provided in the selection list or create your own (e.g., Premier Bank).
6. Determine the type of account to be set up. Select **Savings**.
7. Enter an account number if available, otherwise leave blank.
8. Enter the balance of this account (e.g., $5,300).
9. If no other accounts are available at this institution, select **next** to allow MS Money to set up this account.
10. For the remaining accounts, enter the corresponding data in accordance with the above procedures.

How to prepare a personal balance sheet in Quicken:
1. At the top of the screen, click **File** then **New**.
2. Select **New Quicken Account.**
3. Select **Savings** account.
4. In the associated **Account Name** text box, enter name of account (e.g., Maia's Savings).
5. In the associated **Financial Institution** text box, determine if the institution is provided in the selection list or enter Premier Bank.
6. Select the **Summary** tab at the top of the inner window to enter the savings account balance. Enter $5,300, and then click **Done**.
7. Perform the same steps above for establishing the account balances for the other accounts.
8. Enter the corresponding data in accordance with the above procedures.

Activity 2

In Activity 1 you prepared a personal balance sheet for Maia Lazarus. Maia has never had a budget and she is concerned that she is not saving enough money to meet her goals. She would like to buy a house and travel to Europe. In addition to the monthly expenses listed in the previous activity, Maia estimates that her other monthly expenses include $275 for utilities, $350 for food, $500 for travel and entertainment, $200 for clothing, and $200 for gas. Insurance for her sport utility vehicle is $100 per month, and she contributes $100 to her church each month. After she has $300 transferred to savings, the $144 remaining is used for unexpected expenses.

REQUIRED: Use the information in Activity 1 and this activity to prepare a monthly budget for Maia Lazarus. Remove FORM 2, page 59 for preparing the monthly budget.

Software Directions

How to prepare a monthly budget in Microsoft Money:
1. At the top of the screen, click **Planner.**
2. Under the headline, "tasks you do most often" select **create a budget.**
3. On the left-hand side of the screen, click **Income.**
4. Click **Add category** in the bottom left corner.
5. Select the category **Other income.** Add a new subcategory called **Expense reimbursement.**
6. **Finish** to add the new category to the budget.
7. Utilize and select the **Wages and Salary: Net Pay** for entering monthly income. Remove all other accounts.
8. On the left-hand side of the screen, click **Expenses.**
9. Enter the total monthly expense amounts for each corresponding category.
10. On the left-hand side of the screen, select **monthly summary** to review the monthly budget.

How to prepare a monthly budget in Quicken:
1. At the top of the screen, click **Planning,** then **Budgeting.**
2. Under the left-hand side of the screen, select **categories** and checkmark all the individual categories necessary for preparing the budget, then click on **OK.**
3. Within the budgeting worksheet, select the **options** menu on the right-hand side of the screen.
4. Under the options menu click **Display Months.**
5. Select the month to input the budget data.
6. Click the category cell and enter the budgeted amount in the corresponding field. Note: all positive amounts appear in black and negative amounts in red.
7. After entering the entire budget, return to the **My Finances** home page. Your budget will be saved automatically.

Critical Thinking   If Maia wants to save $500 a month instead of $300 a month, where could she reduce her spending?

_____

_____

_____

_____

_____

_____

_____

_____

Activity 3

Len Lombardo just opened a checking account at First National Bank of Daytona Beach. Below is a record of the activity for the first month that Len had his checking account.

REQUIRED: Complete deposit slips, write checks, and record all checking account transactions for the month in Len's check register. Make sure you enter a description in the register so Len's financial records can be completed. This activity requires 11 checks (#101-111), two deposit slips, and a check register, all located in the last section of this manual. Detach these documents from this manual before starting. Place the documents in the IN FILE for easy access. Once written, checks and deposit slips are placed in the OUT FILE. The check register remains in the IN FILE.

April 1 Len deposited his monthly paycheck for $2,560 to open the account. Fill out a deposit slip for this transaction. The deposit slip from page 137 of this manual should be in your IN FILE along with checks and the check register. The ABA (American Bankers Association) numbers to use in the space provided on the deposit slip are 12-24 (See ABA number 13-42 in Figure 1.1). Remember to record the deposit in the check register. When the deposit slip is completed, place it in the OUT FILE. (Use this procedure each time you prepare a deposit slip.)

April 4 Len bought groceries at Albertson's. Write check #101 for $74.53. Remove the check, obtained earlier from page 129 of this manual, from the IN FILE. Always record the check in the check register before writing the check. Once the check is written, place it in the OUT FILE.

April 5 Len sent his monthly car payment to Sun Coast Credit Union. Write check #102 for $256.

April 5 Len withdrew $100 from an ATM.

April 8 Len received his telephone bill from Southern Bell Telephone Company. Write check #103. Remove FORM 3, page 61 of this manual. Write check #103 for the amount due. File the customer's part of the FORM 3 in the IN FILE. File the return part of the FORM with the check in the OUT FILE. (File all similar forms in this manner.)

April 9 Len joined Fit-For-Life Health Club. Write check #104 in the amount of $35 for his monthly dues.

April 10 Len received his semi-annual premium notice, FORM 4, page 61, for car insurance from Geico. Write check #105. File the form in the IN FILE and the check in the OUT FILE. (File all similar forms in this manner.)

April 12 Len withdrew $200 from an ATM.

Table 1.9

First National Bank of Daytona Beach 352 Gulf Drive South Daytona Beach, FL 32179 Date: May 10, 20--			Len Lombardo 1795 Ocean View Drive Daytona Beach, FL 32016 Account No. 410307056204	
Beginning Balance	Total Payments	Total Deposits	Ending Balance	
-0-	1,957.53	3,365.17	1,407.64	
Date	Check. No.	Amount Paid	Amount Deposited	Balance
4-1			2,560.00	2,560.00
4-5	ATM	100.00		2,460.00
4-7	101	74.53		2,385.47
4-10	103	65.40		2,320.07
4-11	102	256.00		2,064.07
4-12	ATM	200.00		
	Fee	1.75		1,862.32
4-14	104	35.00		1,827.32
4-14	105	375.00		1,452.32
4-15			802.00	2,254.32
4-20	107	535.01		1,719.31
4-22	ATM	100.00		1,619.31
4-26	109	83.32		1,535.99
4-27	108	131.52		1,404.47
4-30			Int. 3.17	1,407.64

How many ATM withdrawals are included on his bank statement? How much did he withdraw?
Answer: Three withdrawals equaling $400.00

April 15 Len contributed to United Way of Volusia County. Write check #106 for $75.

April 15 Len received a check, FORM 5, page 63, from the U. S. Treasury for a tax refund. Remove the check and deposit it in his account. Fill in a deposit slip for this deposit. Remember to include the two ABA numbers (12–47) located on the check in the space provided on the deposit slip.

April 17 Len bought an ocean kayak from East Coast Outdoors. Write check #107 for $535.01.

April 19 Len received his electric bill, FORM 6, page 63, from Florida Power & Light. Write check #108.

April 20 Len bought groceries at Albertson's. Write check #109 for $83.32.

April 22 Len withdrew $100 from an ATM.

April 24 Len sent a check to Daytona Shoestring Theater for two tickets to Miss Firecracker. Write check #110 for $70.

April 26 Len received his monthly cable bill, FORM 7, page 63, from Halifax Cable Company. Write check #111.

April 30 Len withdrew $200 from an ATM.

Critical Thinking   In which one of these transactions is Len buying an asset?

_____

_____

_____

_____

_____

_____

_____

_____

———————Activity 4———————

Using the information in Activity 3, reconcile Len Lombardo's April bank statement. The bank statement is shown in Table 1.9, page 11. Use FORM 8, page 65 to prepare Len's Bank Reconciliation Form.

Software Directions

How to prepare a bank reconciliation in Microsoft Money:
1. At the top of the screen, click **Accounts**.
2. Set up a new account.
3. Select the account to record the monthly activity.
4. Enter the date and transaction into the account at the bottom of the screen.
5. Select **category**, **subcategory**, and press **enter**.
6. For each subsequent daily activity, record the proper withdrawal, deposit, or transfer amount.

How to prepare a bank reconciliation in Quicken:
1. Open the account register that you want to reconcile. At the top of the screen, click **Banking**, then **Banking Activities**, and **Enter a transaction into my register.**
2. Using Len Lombardo's check register, check the opening balance, input that number, and then enter his ending balance.
3. Continue to enter the date, amount, and categorical information, and then press **enter**. Remember to enter all service charges or interest earned as indicated on statement.

4. When finished clearing each transaction then click **Reconcile**, look at the **Difference** at the bottom of the screen. If the difference amount is zero then you have reconciled Len Lombardo's account.

A COMPREHENSIVE PROBLEM

Earlier in this unit you read about Jerome Roberts' financial activity. Roommate Josh Adams wants Jerome to help him prepare a budget and show him how to keep track of his spending.

Josh attends California Community College on an academic scholarship so his tuition and books are paid for, however, he doesn't make enough money from his part-time job as a math tutor to pay his expenses. At the beginning of the semester, Josh took out a student loan to help pay his expenses while attending college.

Jerome and Josh discovered that their monthly expenses were similar. Josh also knows how to reconcile a bank statement and keeps receipts for most of his expenses. Jerome explained to Josh how important it is to keep track of all his expenses, especially his out-of-pocket expenses.

REQUIRED: Using the following information, complete this activity's six steps:
1. Prepare a personal balance sheet for Josh.
2. Prepare a monthly budget for Josh.
3. Reconcile Josh's bank statement.
4. Prepare a cash record sheet for Josh.
5. Prepare a financial record sheet for Josh.
6. Prepare a budget comparison sheet for Josh.

Step 1: Josh maintains a savings, checking, and loan account at the California Community College Credit Union. Josh has $8,800 in savings, and $5,000 of this money is from the proceeds of his short-term student loan. Josh's ending checking account balance for November is $545.50. His other assets include an old Ford Taurus valued at $3,300 (purchase price: $3,700), a computer valued at $800, furniture valued at $2,500, and other assets valued at $1,500. Josh's only liability is the $5,000 student loan. Prepare a personal balance sheet for Josh using FORM 9, page 67.

Software Directions

How to prepare a personal balance sheet with Microsoft Money:
1. At the top of the screen, click **Accounts**.

2. On the left-hand side of the screen, click **Set up accounts.**
3. Click **Add a new account.**
4. In the associated text box, enter account is held at the California Community College Credit Union.
5. Determine if the institution is provided in the selection list or select **use California Community College Credit Union.**
6. Determine the type of account to be set up. For this example, select **Savings.**
7. Call this account **California Community Col Savings.**
8. Enter an account number if available, otherwise leave blank.
9. Enter **$8,800 US Dollars** for the opening balance of this account.
10. As there are **other accounts available at this institution,** enter both the $545.50 **checking account** and $5,000 **student loan liability** account information accordingly.
11. No other accounts are available at this institution. Select **next** to allow MS Money to set up this account.
12. Electronic bill paying is not available for this institution. Select **finish** to create your account.
13. For the remaining asset accounts (i.e., $3,300 Ford Taurus **Asset,** $800 Computer **Asset,** $2,500 Furniture **Asset,** and $1,500 Other **Assets**) enter the corresponding data in accordance with the above procedures. Note that these particular assets are not held at a bank, brokerage, or other financial institution.

How to prepare a personal balance sheet in Quicken:
1. At the top of the screen, click **File** then **New.**
2. Select **New Quicken Account.**
3. Select **Savings** account. Click **Next.**
4. In the associated **Account Name** text box, enter **California Community College Savings.**
5. In the associated **Financial Institution** text box, determine if the institution is provided in the selection list or enter **California Community College Credit Union.**
6. Select the **Summary** tab at the top of the inner window to enter the savings account balance of $8,800 with a date of 12/01/00. Click **Done.**

7. Perform the same steps above for establishing the account balances for the checking and student loan liability accounts at this particular institution.
8. For the remaining asset accounts (i.e., $3,300 Ford Taurus **Asset,** $800 Computer **Asset,** $2,500 Furniture **Asset,** and $1,500 Other **Assets**) enter the corresponding data in accordance with the above procedures. Note that these particular assets are not held at a bank, brokerage, or other financial institution.

Step 2: Josh used Jerome's budget to help estimate his monthly expenses of rent ($700), food ($200), leisure and entertainment ($100), telephone ($50), and electric ($100). He also estimates that he spends $100 a month on clothing, $80 a month on gas, and $145 a month on miscellaneous expenses. Josh's parents are paying for his car insurance while he is in college and his student loan payments do not begin until he graduates.

Josh received reimbursement from Jerome for one-half of his rent, telephone, and electric expenses. He estimates this reimbursement to be about $425 each month. Josh earns about $550 a month take-home pay tutoring math. The withdrawal from his savings account covers the rest of his expenses. To determine the amount of withdrawal from savings, subtract the totals of $425 (Jerome's reimbursement) and $550 (Josh's take-home pay) from total expenses. He plans to work full-time in the summer to replenish his savings account. Prepare a monthly budget for Josh using FORM 10, page 69.

Software Directions
How to prepare a monthly budget in Microsoft Money:
1. At the top of the screen, click **Planner.**
2. Under the headline, "tasks you do most often" select **create a budget.**
3. On the left-hand side of the screen, click **Income.**
4. Click **add category…** in the bottom left corner.
5. Select the category **other income.** Add a new subcategory called **expense reimbursement.**
6. **Finish** to add the new category to the budget.
7. Utilize the **Wages and Salary: Net Pay** for entering Josh's monthly income received from

Table 1.10

JOSH ADAM'S CHECK REGISTER

Check No.	Date	Checks Issued To or Description of Deposit	Payments	✓	Deposit	Balance
						545.50
	12-1	Deposit—From Savings			500.00	1,045.50
101	12-1	First Class Properties	700.00			345.50
	12-5	ATM Withdrawal	200.00			145.00
	12-5	Deposit—1/2 Rent from Jerome			350.00	495.50
	12-13	ATM Withdrawal	200.00			295.50
	12-15	Deposit—Paycheck			258.10	553.60
	12-28	ATM Withdrawal	200.00			353.60
102	12-28	California Power and Light	88.00			265.60
103	12-28	California Bell	64.00			201.60
	12-28	Deposit—1/2 Electric & Phone from Jerome			76.00	277.60
	12-31	Deposit—Paycheck			302.90	580.50

Table 1.11

JOSH ADAM'S BANK STATEMENT

CALIFORNIA COMMUNITY COLLEGE CREDIT UNION CARMEL, CA 95286	Josh Adams Student PO Box 30234 California Community College Carmel, CA 95286

Date: January 9, 20--   Account No. 5300059002

Beginning Balance	Total Payments	Total Deposits	Ending Balance
545.50	1,305.00	1,108.10	348.60

Date	Check No.	Amount Paid	Amount Deposited	Balance
12-1			500.00	1,045.50
12-5	ATM	200.00		845.50
12-6			350.00	1,195.50
12-7	101	700.00		495.50
12-13	ATM	200.00		295.50
12-15			258.10	553.60
12-28	ATM	200.00		353.60
12-29	Fee	5.00		348.60

tutoring. Remove all other accounts. Select **other income: expense reimbursement** and in the bottom right corner under the headline, "In this category, I expect to receive" enter **$425 every month.**

8. Select **Wages and Salary: Net Pay** and enter **$550 every month.**

9. On the left-hand side of the screen, click **Expenses.**

10. Eliminate all expense accounts except for Automobile: Gasoline, Bills: Electricity, Bills: Rent, Bills: Telephone, Clothing: [all], Food: Groceries, Leisure: [all], and **All Other Expenses.**

11. Enter the total monthly expense amounts for each corresponding category.

12. On the left-hand side of the screen, select **monthly summary** to review the monthly budget for Josh.

How to prepare a monthly budget in Quicken:

1. At the top of the screen, click **Planning** and then **Budgeting.**

2. Under the left-hand side of the screen, select **categories** and checkmark all the individual categories necessary for preparing the budget for Josh (i.e., **Other Inc, Salary, Fuel, Clothing, Entertainment, Groceries, Misc., Rent, Gas and Electric, Telephone, To Checking** and **From Savings**) and click on **OK.**

3. Within the budgeting worksheet, select the **Options** menu on the upper right-hand side of the screen.

4. Under the options menu click **Display Months.**

5. Select the month of December to input the budget data.

6. Click the category cell and enter the budgeted amount in the corresponding field. Note that all positive amounts appear in black and negative amounts in red.

7. After entering the entire budget, return to the **My Finances** home page. Your budget will be saved automatically.

Step 3: As of November 30, all Josh's checks had cleared the bank and his checkbook balance had matched his bank balance of $545.50. Josh's check register for his checking account for December is shown in Table 1.10. December's bank statement for his checking account is shown in Table 1.11. Using FORM 11, page 71, prepare a bank reconciliation form for Josh.

Software Directions

How to prepare a bank reconciliation in Microsoft Money:
1. At the top of the screen, click **Accounts**.
2. Select the checking account to record the monthly activity.
3. Select the **deposit** tab located at the bottom of the screen.
4. Enter the 12/1 deposit from savings of $500.
5. Select category **transfer**, subcategory **Community College Savings** and press **enter**.
6. Next, select the **withdrawal** tab to record the $700 rental payment to First Class Properties.
7. Enter check **number 101** in the number text box.
8. Select **bills** as a category for the payment and **rent** as a subcategory.
9. For each subsequent daily activity, record the proper withdrawal, deposit, or transfer amount.

How to prepare a bank reconciliation in Quicken:
1. Open the account register that you want to reconcile. At the top of the screen, choose **Banking**, then **Banking Activities**, and **Enter a transaction into my register.**
2. Click **Reconcile** on the tool bar.
3. Using Josh Adams' check register, check the opening balance, input that number, and then enter his ending balance.
4. Continue to enter the date, amount, and categorical information, and then enter **OK**. Remember to enter all service charges or interest earned if necessary.

5. When finished clearing each transaction, look at the **Difference** in the reconciliation box. If the difference amount is zero then you have reconciled Josh Adams' account.

Step 4: The following is a list of Josh's out-of-pocket expenses for December. Using this information, complete his cash record sheet (FORM 12, page 73), for December (make sure you enter the ATM withdrawals from his checkbook register).

12-5	Josh used $25.00 to fill up his car and spent $55.60 on groceries.
12-9	Josh spent $50.50 on tickets to a motor cross race.
12-12	Josh spent $12.50 on dinner.
12-13	Josh bought a pair of shoes for $78.20.
12-16	Josh spent $12 on a movie and $115.00 on groceries.
12-18	Josh used $26.50 to fill up his car and spent $7.75 on lunch.
12-28	Josh spent $20 on tickets to a basketball game and $8.50 on snacks.
12-29	Josh bought his girlfriend a $50 gift certificate for the mall and spent $57.20 on groceries.
12-31	Josh paid $35 for tickets to a concert and spent $17.20 on food.

Step 5: After you complete Josh's cash record sheet, prepare his financial record sheet (FORM 13, page 75) Remember to use his checkbook register, bank reconciliation form, and cash record sheet in preparing his financial record sheet.

Software Directions

How to prepare a financial record sheet in a spreadsheet program:
1. Select **File** and **New** to begin a new workbook.
2. Begin by entering each column title in the top row.
3. Select an entire column by clicking the column letter noted in gray and move the mouse over the column edge until a crosshatch appears. Pressing and holding the left mouse button, adjust the column width to your desired specifications, or double-click the button on the edge of the column to automatically fit each column.

4. For each row, enter the daily activity into the designated column for each particular column classification.

5. After entering the daily activity into the workbook, find the sum of the totals of each column by selecting the cell under the final entry of each column. Click on the summation symbol (Σ) at the top of the toolbar. Select all activity in the corresponding column for summation.

6. Finally, double underline all totals in the workbook to designate that each cell is a summation of the activity above. Utilize the underline tool on the formatting toolbar at the top of your screen. To activate the formatting tool bar, hover the mouse pointer over the top of the screen and right click. Select **Format Cells.** Choose the type of underline as needed.

Step 6: Now that Josh's financial records are complete for December, he wants to know how his estimated and actual income, expenses, and savings compare. Prepare Josh's budget comparison sheet (FORM 14, page 77) for December.

Software Directions
How to prepare a budget comparison in Microsoft Money:
1. At the top of the screen, click **accounts.**
2. Select the **checking account.**
3. On the left-hand side of the screen, click **Analyze Spending and View all available reports.**
4. Click the report titled **How I'm Doing on My Budget.**
5. Compare the Budget to Actual details.

How to prepare a budget comparison in Quicken:
1. Click **Reports** menu, **Reports and Graphs Center.** Select a category from the list of topics. Click on the report you want to create.
2. Select the date range you want to include in the budget report.
3. Click **Create Now.**
4. Compare the report to your actual details.

Critical Thinking   Are the variances favorable or unfavorable on Josh's budget comparison sheet? Was his budget realistic? Should he revise his budget for next month? Can you think of ways Josh can use less of his savings each month to meet his expenses?

_____
_____
_____
_____
_____
_____
_____
_____
_____
_____
_____
_____
_____
_____
_____
_____
_____
_____
_____
_____
_____
_____
_____
_____
_____
_____
_____
_____
_____
_____

The Young Married Couple

After completing this unit, you will be able to:

- Calculate interest.

- Define credit cards and calculate finance charges on credit cards.

- Define installment loans.

- Select appropriate life insurance.

- Calculate out-of-pocket expenses on health insurance.

- Select appropriate motor vehicle insurance.

- Compare and contrast savings accounts.

isagreements over finances often cause the most tension between married couples. Ann and Rick Miller are now aware of this. They married less than a year ago in Miami on the beach. Everything was perfect, right down to the appetizers at the reception and the balmy breeze. After the honeymoon they moved to Ormond Beach, Florida, where Ann accepted a teaching position at Seabreeze High School, and Rick transferred with Greer Construction Company.

Rick worked long hours as well as studied for his general contractor's license, so Ann decided it was a good opportunity for her to start a master of education program, since the school district offered a nice increase in her salary after receiving the advanced degree. She decided to enroll at Stetson University in DeLand since she could obtain a certificate as a reading specialist. The only bad part was that the university was 30 minutes away from home.

On the weekends they vowed to spend every moment together. Usually they went hiking, camping, or fishing. On occasion they went scuba diving. During their outdoor excursions they often talked about their future, and inevitably, money issues entered the conversation. When they were single each of them had their own way of handling finances—Ann used any extra monies to pay off her student loan, and Rick always believed in saving money although he kept a balance on his credit cards and paid installments on his truck loan, which was five years old. They were both stubborn about their own method of handling finances so they decided to take a closer look at their financial situation together.

The Millers Learn to Calculate Interest

The Millers decide it is too early in their relationship for finances to cause arguments. They decide to attend a basic financial planning course offered at their church. The course is designed for young married couples. It is geared for couples to assess their past financial decisions and to set new goals together. The first topic discussed in the seminar is **interest**—a fee for borrowing money. If you deposit money in a savings account at the

bank, the bank pays you a fee for the use of your money. The bank is borrowing money from you. For example, Rick has a truck loan and a credit card balance, which means he is paying the

Table 2.1

ANN AND RICK MILLER PERSONAL BALANCE SHEET
December 31

ASSETS		
Checking Account	$ 1,350	
Savings–Rick	8,300	
Savings–Ann	600	
Car	2,200	
Truck	7,500	
Furniture	1,200	
Total Assets		$21,150
LIABILITIES		
Truck Loan	$ 6,200	
Sears Credit Card	3,850	
Dillards Credit Card	2,600	
Visa Credit Card	4,200	
Total Liabilities		$16,850
NET WORTH		4,300
Total Liabilities and Net Worth		$21,150

If the Millers didn't have a Visa balance, what would be their total liabilities as of December 31?
Answer: $12,650.

lenders interest for borrowing their money.

They learn about two types of interest: simple interest and compound interest. **Simple interest** is interest paid only on the deposited amount or original amount of the loan. **Compound interest** is interest paid on the deposited amount and on previously earned interest. On loans, compound interest is calculated more than once during the period of the loan.

The amount of interest paid by a borrower depends on three factors: 1) how much money is being borrowed, 2) the percent of interest charged on the loan, and 3) the length of time of the loan. The amount of money being borrowed is called the **principal**. The percent of interest charged on the loan is called the *rate*. The duration of the loan is called the *time*.

The simple interest formula is: INTEREST = PRINCIPAL × RATE × TIME. When using this

TABLE OF COMMON INTEREST RATES AND DECIMAL EQUIVALENTS

5% = .05	8% = .08	12% = .12
5¼% = .0525	8¼% = .0825	12¼% = .1225
5½% = .055	8½% = .085	12½% = .125
5¾% = .0575	8¾% = .0875	12¾% = .1275

What is 5 3/4 percent equivalent to in a decimal form?
Answer: .0575

formula the rate is stated as a decimal. For example, seven percent is represented as .07 and seven and a half percent is .075. A table of common rates and their decimal equivalents is shown in Table 2.2.

The simple interest formula expresses time in years or fractions of a year. For instance, a loan for two years would be two. If the loan were for six months then the time would be a half or sixth-twelfths because six months is one-half or sixth-twelfths of a year. Ann's savings account is earning three and a half percent simple interest. To find the amount of interest she earns in one year multiply the principal ($600) by the rate (.035) by the time (1). $600 × .035 × 1 = $21.

There are two ways to calculate the time factor for simple interest when the time is stated in days. The **exact interest method** uses 365 days as the denominator of the fraction. For example, if you put $2,000 into a savings account for 73 days and the bank paid six percent exact interest, you would earn $24 ($2,000 × .06 × 73/365). The second method is the **ordinary interest method** and uses a denominator of 360. This method was common before computers and calculators were invented because it was easier to use. If you deposit $1,500 in a savings account for 90 days and the bank pays you four percent ordinary interest, you earn $15 ($1,500 × .04 × 90/360).

The Millers' Open-End Credit

A *credit card* is a card issued by a bank or private company that allows you to "buy now and pay later." Most credit cards allow you to make both small and large purchases up to a specified limit. This specified limit is called your *credit limit* and is the maximum amount of debt that a borrower can have on a particular credit card at any one time. With credit cards you usually have the option of paying the balance off each month or making a smaller payment toward the balance. You can continue to charge purchases even

though your balance is not paid off as long as you don't exceed your credit limit.

Ann's credit card is shown in Figure 2.1.

Credit cards of this type are called **open-end credit** because there are no fixed payments and you just continue paying and charging as long as your account remains open.

Hanson Credit Inc.
1378 Lane Towers, Suite 2
Atlanta, GA 30304

5329 0616 2008 5062

Valid Thru: 05/02/03

ANN MILLER   Cardholder Since: 2000

What is the expiration date on Ann Miller's credit card?
Answer: 05/02/03.

CREDIT CARDS

As with other types of loans, credit card balances cost the borrower money. The **finance charge** is the dollar amount that is paid for credit. The **annual percentage rate** (APR) is the true annual interest rate being charged for credit. Both the finance charge and the APR must be disclosed to the borrower in writing. You can find the **monthly finance rate** by dividing the APR by 12. For example, if the APR is 24 percent the monthly finance rate is two percent (24% ÷ 12). If you decide to apply for a credit card find out the rate you will be paying for

Keywords

Interest – fee for borrowing money.
Simple interest – interest paid only on the deposited amount or original amount.
Compound interest – interest paid on previously earned interest as well as the original deposit.
Principal – amount of money being borrowed.
Exact interest method – uses 365 days as the base (denominator) of the fraction for time in computing interest.
Ordinary interest method – uses 360 days as the base (denominator) of the fraction for time in computing interest.
Open-end credit – no fixed payments and the borrower can keep charging and paying as long as the account remains open and the borrower stays within the credit limit.
Finance charge – dollar amount that is paid for credit.
Annual percentage rate (APR) – true annual interest rate being charged for credit.
Monthly finance rate – APR divided by 12.

Table 2.3

CREDIT CARD STATEMENT FOR THE MILLERS

Hanson Credit, Inc.
CREDIT CARD STATEMENT

Acct. No. 6498-7723-4432   Ann and Rick Miller
Billing Cycle: June 1–30   15 Ocean Lane
                                   Ormond Beach, FL 32074

DATE	PURCHASE	PAYMENT	BALANCE
June 1			$2,000
June 15	$38		$2,038
June 23		$2,000	$38
June 28	$289		$327

Remit full amount or minimum payment of $40 before July 10, 20-- to Hanson Credit, Inc., 1378 Lane Towers, Suite 2, Atlanta, GA 30304.

Thank you!

What is the balance due on the credit card as of June 15?
Answer: $2,038.

credit. Rates vary widely and depend on many factors including competitors' rates, the demand for credit, and the type of card for which you are applying.

When you apply for a credit card or for any other type of loan, the lender will check your credit rating. A *credit rating* is a system of evaluating whether a potential borrower is likely to pay the loan. Some of the factors that will be taken into consideration are your history of paying loans and credit cards on time, your current debt load, your income and job stability, and your personal assets. The lender can find this information about you at any one of three major credit bureaus. A *credit bureau* is a company that gathers information on borrowers and provides this information to lenders.

When you have a credit card you usually receive a monthly bill. At the end of the billing period, the company that issued the credit card sends you a statement that shows your purchases, payments, and finance charge. This statement is sent to you on the same date each month but not necessarily at the end of the month. It is important that you check all the activity on your account to make sure it's accurate. A credit card statement for Ann and Rick is shown in Table 2.3.

There are two ways to calculate finance charges on credit cards: the unpaid balance method and the average daily balance method. The first method, the **unpaid balance method**, uses the ending balance from the previous month's statement to calculate the finance charge. To calculate the

finance charge using this method, simply multiply the ending balance on your last statement by the monthly finance charge rate. For example, if your Visa account had an unpaid balance of $1,500 on January 31 and the monthly rate was one percent, your finance charge on your February statement would be $15 ($1,500 × .01). Now suppose during February you made purchases of $25, $150, and $75. You also made a payment of $200. What would the finance charge be on your March statement? First, find the ending balance for February ($1,500 + $15 + $25 + $150 + $75 − $200 = $1,565. Then, multiply the ending balance ($1,550) by the monthly finance charge rate (one percent). The answer is $15.50 ($1,550 × .01).

Most companies use the second method, **average daily balance method**, to calculate finance charges. Use these steps to calculate the finance charge for this method:

1. Find the balance at the end of each day in the billing period.
2. Add the amounts in step one.
3. Divide the sum found in step two by the number of days in the billing period.
4. Multiply the difference in step three by the monthly finance charge rate.

Table 2.4 illustrates the computation of the average daily balance method.

Rick has three credit cards with ongoing monthly balances. The interest rate on his Sears card is one and three-fourths percent per month and the interest rate on his Visa is one and a half percent a month. Both of these companies use the average daily balance method to calculate the finance charge. Rick's Dillards credit card interest rate is one percent per month, and they use the unpaid balance method to calculate the finance charge.

THEIR INSTALLMENT LOAN

An **installment loan** is a lump sum loan that is paid off with a series of equal monthly payments. These types of loans are used to buy vehicles, boats, appliances, computers, and even services such as vacations and education. On most installment loans the borrower makes a *down payment* in cash and finances the remaining balance of the

Table 2.4

COMPUTATION OF THE AVERAGE DAILY BALANCE METHOD

DATE	PURCHASE	PAYMENT	BALANCE*
6-1	$ 500		$1,500
6-20	$ 200		$1,700
6-26	$ 50		$1,750
6-30		$1,000	$ 750

Step 1: Days balance was $1,500 = 19
Days balance was $1,700 = 6
Days balance was $1,750 = 4
Days balance was $ 750 = 1
30 (days in billing period)

Step 2: $1,500 × 19 = $28,500
$1,700 × 6 = $10,200
$1,750 × 4 = $ 7,000
$ 750 × 1 = $ 750
$46,450 (total of each day's balance)

Step 3: $46,450 ÷ 30 = $1,548.33 (average daily balance)

Step 4: $1,548.33 × .015 = $23.22 (monthly finance charge)

*Assume on 5-30, the credit card balance is $1,000; the monthly finance rate is 1½ percent.

price of a good or service. The down payment is usually a certain percentage of the purchase price. For example, you might buy a new car for $16,000 and put 20 percent down, financing the balance. The amount of your down payment is $3,200 ($16,000 × .20). The *amount financed* is the purchase price minus the down payment ($16,000 − $3,200 = $12,800). The lender then adds the finance charge to the amount financed to get the *total amount of installment payments*. Once the total amount of installment payments is calculated, divide this amount by the number of months in the loan to get the *monthly payment*. For example, a 36-month loan with a total amount of installment payments of $4,500 would have monthly payments of $125 ($4,500 ÷ 36). To find the *total costs of the purchase* add the down payment to the total amount of installment payments. For example, a friend of the Millers purchased a new leather recliner paying $100 down and financing the balance for 12 months. The payments are $42 a month. The total cost of their friend's purchase is $604 ($100 + 12 × $42).

Ann and Rick have one installment loan—Rick's truck. Rick pays $310 a month on this loan and has 20 payments left. The APR is eight percent.

ANN AND RICK'S INSURANCE

Everyone faces the possibility of loss that can result in unfavorable financial consequences. Whether it is inclement weather damaging your home, a car accident, or a lawsuit, it is imperative to have insurance to protect you against these losses. Your insurance needs will change as your living and working situations change. Almost anything can be insured (musicians and surgeons even insure their hands). Typical insurance falls into four main categories: life, health, motor vehicle, and home.

Life Insurance

There are two basic types of life insurance: term insurance and cash value policy. **Term insurance** provides income to your designated beneficiaries when you die. The term is the number of years for which you are covered. Term insurance is usually sold in increments of $1,000 and the *premium*, which is the amount you pay each month for the insurance, depends on your age and the amount of the policy. Some term insurance policies are set up to renew annually and your premiums change each year. Other term insurance policies have premiums that don't change. Annual renewable term insurance usually starts off with low premiums and the premiums increase as you get older. Level premium policies start with higher premiums but the premiums do not increase.

Term insurance can be set up in a number of ways. Some policies pay out a specific amount, for example, $50,000 at any time the insured per-

Keywords

Unpaid balance method – uses the ending balance from the previous month's statement to calculate the finance charge.
Average daily balance method – uses the balance each day of the billing cycle to calculate the finance charge.
Installment loan – lump sum loan that is paid off with a series of equal monthly payments.
Term insurance – provides income to your designated beneficiaries if you die during the term of the policy.

son dies during the coverage period. Other term insurance policies pay decreasing amounts, as the insured person gets older.

Cash value policies serve two purposes. First, they pay a certain amount to your beneficiary if you die. (A **beneficiary** is a person named on an insurance policy to receive the benefits.) Second, cash value policies build up a cash value that you can collect before you die. These policies serve as both insurance and as an investment. If you choose a cash value policy, understand that the rate on the investment portion is usually very low compared to other types of investments. Cash value policies are also more expensive than term insurance.

When you consider buying life insurance ask yourself the following questions:

1. Do I have adequate financial resources to provide for my burial?
2. Will I need part of my insurance to settle my debts after I die?
3. Do I have enough money in savings and investments to provide any needed support for my surviving family members?

Ann has a life insurance policy through the Volusia County school system. If she dies, the policy pays her survivor two times her annual salary. There is no cash value and the policy is terminated if she leaves her job. Rick doesn't have life insurance.

Health Insurance

Health insurance protects you if you get sick. Most health insurance policies cover hospital stays, visits to a doctor, medical tests, and prescription drugs. Many people get health insurance through their employer as an employee benefit. This type of health insurance is called **group insurance.**

When you evaluate a potential group health insurance plan, you should consider several factors. First, how much of your monthly premium does your employer pay?

This amount can range from 0 to 100 percent and your premium might be several hundred dollars a month. Next, find out exactly what is covered. Some policies are set up so that only a particular network of doctors and hospitals can be used. This type of system is called a **health maintenance organization** (HMO). Other policies allow you to use any medical provider but they can be much more expensive.

Next, find out your annual deductible and out-of-pocket expenses for the plan. Your *annual*

deductible is the amount you are expected to pay each year before your medical coverage starts. This can range from a few hundred dollars to a few thousand dollars. For example, if your annual deductible is $500, you must pay the first $500 of medical expenses before your insurance will pay anything.

Coinsurance is a percentage of each medical expense that you are expected to pay. If you visit a dermatologist or any other specialist, you might have to pay a flat coinsurance payment of $30, no matter what the doctor actually charges. If the specialist cost $150, you would pay $30 and your insurance would pay $120 ($150 − $30). Sometimes coinsurance requires you to pay a percentage rather than a flat dollar amount. In the last example, if you had a 25 percent coinsurance requirement, you would pay $37.50 ($150 × .25) and the insurance company would pay $112.50 ($150 − $37.50).

Many insurance policies have an **out-of-pocket maximum** stating that once you have paid out a certain amount of money in a particular year, you will no longer have to pay the coinsurance. From that point on, the insurance company covers the full cost of each medical expense. Sometimes, this out-of-pocket maximum can be quite high. Unfortunately, most policies also have a **lifetime maximum**. This is a limit on the total amount that they will pay for one person over a lifetime. A common lifetime maximum is one million dollars.

Always find out if your spouse and children are covered under your plan and, if so, at what cost to you. If both you and your spouse are covered by separate health plans, it's important to coordinate benefits and make sure at least one of the policies covers your children adequately.

If you terminate employment with a particular company you have the right to continue your group insurance for up to 18 months. However, you must pay the full cost of the insurance.

If your employer doesn't offer insurance, you need to find an individual plan. These plans work just like group plans but are usually much more expensive. An HMO covers Ann and Rick through her school district, but does not provide coverage for dental and vision claims. This means that trips to the dentist, eye exams, glasses, and contact lenses are paid out-of-pocket by Ann and Rick.

Ann's employer also provides them with disability insurance. Disability insurance is insurance designed to pay you income if you become permanently disabled. Ann's policy will pay 50 percent of her salary for 10 years if she becomes permanently disabled. Rick does not have disability insurance.

Motor Vehicle Insurance

Many states require you to have insurance on your car. The cost of auto insurance depends on your age, marital status, where you live, what kind of car you drive, how far you drive each year, and your driving record (including accidents and tickets). Auto insurance covers both property (your car) and liability (damage to other people and their property). Some states require more insurance than others. There are at least six major parts to an auto insurance policy. Below is a brief description of each part.

- Bodily injury liability—provides insurance if you kill or injure someone.
- Property damage—covers damage you do to someone's car or other property.
- Collision—covers damage to your car.
- Comprehensive—protects your auto against theft or damages caused by something other than a collision.
- Medical payments—covers medical expenses of you and passengers in your car
- Uninsured motorists—covers injuries to you and passengers in your car if someone who doesn't have insurance hits you.

ANN AND RICK'S SAVINGS

Ann and Rick would like to save more money so they can buy Ann a new car and buy a home. They know savings is also about extra cash in case of an emergency (e.g., unemployment). Savings accounts at banks and credit unions are low-interest rate accounts. Even at low rates of interest, savings accounts attract many depositors because the money can be withdrawn at any time and most savings accounts are insured so they are low risk. If you have your money in an insured account, you are protected (up to $100,000) if the bank is out of funds to pay depositors. Most savings accounts have a minimum balance requirement, such as $50. You can withdraw and deposit money as long as you maintain the minimum balance.

A **money market account** is a form of savings account that pays a slightly higher rate of interest but requires a higher minimum balance.

A **certificate of deposit (CD)** is similar to a savings account in that it is usually insured. The dif-

ference is that you are required to keep your money on deposit for a specific period of time such as six months or one year with a CD. Usually, the longer the term of the CD, the higher the interest rate. If you decide to withdraw your money before the term ends, you are required to pay a penalty and give up some of your interest.

Ann and Rick also learned about simple interest and compound interest. When interest on a savings account, money market account, or CD is compounded, it amounts to more than when it is paid as simple interest. The more frequent the compounding, the more interest you receive.

The following example shows how compounding affects the amount of interest you receive. Suppose First Security Bank pays eight percent simple interest on a three-year CD and United Federal Credit Union pays eight percent interest, compounded yearly on a three-year CD. Here are the results:

First Security Bank
$$\$50,000 \times .08 \times 3 = \$12,000 \text{ total interest}$$
United Federal Credit Union
$$\$50,000 \times .08 \times 1 = \$ 4,000.00 \text{ first year}$$
$$\$54,000 \times .08 \times 1 = \$ 4,320.00 \text{ second year}$$
$$\$58,320 \times .08 \times 1 = \underline{\$ 4,665.60} \text{ third year}$$
$$\$12,985.60 \text{ total interest}$$

Rick's savings account pays three percent simple interest and Ann's savings account pays two and a half percent simple interest.

Keywords

Cash value policies – pay a certain amount to your beneficiaries if you die and builds up a cash value that you can collect before you die.

Beneficiary – A person named on an insurance policy to receive the benefits or proceeds of the policy.

Group insurance – health insurance offered to a particular group of people.

Health maintenance organization (HMO) – insurance plan whereby the insured is restricted to the use of a particular network of doctors, hospitals, and services.

Out-of-pocket maximum – the maximum amount of money that you are required to pay out-of-pocket in any one year.

Lifetime maximum – limit on the total amount that the insurance company will pay for one person over a lifetime.

Money market account – form of savings account that pays a slightly higher rate of interest but usually requires a higher minimum balance.

Certificate of deposit – account that requires you to keep your money on deposit for a certain length of time and usually pays a higher rate than savings accounts or money market accounts.

Student Activities

INSTRUCTIONS: This section is designed for you to practice the concepts introduced in this unit. In the Student Activities, refer back to this unit if you need help calculating finance charges or down payments or interest, as well as preparing personal balance sheets. Additionally, these activities may be completed by two methods: manually or automatically (e.g., Microsoft Money, Quicken, and Excel). The activities that merit automation include software directions.

You may use the Answer Sheet on page 79 for activities not requiring FORMS. Remove the Answer Sheet before beginning the following activities and place it in your IN FILE. Once you have completed the activities place the Answer Sheet in the OUT FILE. Activities requiring FORMS include the page numbers of the FORMS and are filed appropriately in either the IN FILE or OUT FILE.

Activity 1

A copy of William Shabazz's credit card statement for May is shown in Table 2.5. The annual percentage of 12 percent is calculated on the previous month's balance.

REQUIRED: Use William's credit card statement to calculate the finance charge if the company had used the average daily balance method.

Critical Thinking   Can you think of some reasons most companies use the average daily balance method?

_____

_____

_____

_____

_____

Activity 2

Randall Kajstura found a boat that he wants to buy. The cash price of the boat is $12,500. The boat dealership agreed to finance the boat if Randall put down 20 percent. He would pay the balance, including the finance charge in 60 monthly payments of $200 each.

REQUIRED: What is the amount of the down payment? What is the amount financed? What is the total amount of installment payments? What is the total cost of the boat? What is the finance charge?

Table 2.5

CREDIT CARD STATEMENT FOR WILLIAM SHABAZZ

Hanson Credit, Inc.
CREDIT CARD STATEMENT

Acct. No. 8493-8859-2245
Billing Cycle: May 1–31

William Shabazz
10 Orchard Way
Port Henry, NY 12974

DATE	PURCHASE	PAYMENT	BALANCE
May 1			$3,000
May 15	$ 84		$3,084
May 23		$2,000	$1,084
May 28	$ 309		$1,393

Remit full amount or minimum payment of $40 before June 10, 20-- to Hanson Credit, Inc., 1378 Lane Towers, Suite 2, Atlanta, GA 30304.

Thank you!

What is the billing period for William Shabazz's credit card?
Answer: May 1–31.

Activity 3

Tyrone and Emily Albert both work for Sandlock Publishing Company. Sandlock has a group health insurance plan that covers all its employees. The monthly cost of the plan is $230 for each employee and the company pays $200 of that cost. The annual deductible for each insured person is $500 and the coinsurance payment schedule is listed below:

Primary care physician visit	$10
Specialist physician visit	$20
Prescription drugs	$15
Overnight in hospital	10%
X-rays	$25
Emergency room visits	$50
All other covered procedures	15%

The maximum out-of-pocket expense per individual is $2,500.

REQUIRED: Tyrone and Emily want you to help them prepare a budget to cover their expected out-of-pocket medical expenses. The following lists include Tyrone and Emily's actual medical expenses for last year.

Tyrone met his $500 deductible in May. The following actual charges were incurred after he met his deductible:

May 23   Visit to gastroenterologist $230
May 24   Prescription $102
June 15 Visit to primary care physician for eye infection $75
June 15 Prescription $35
Oct. 20 Trip to emergency room $750
Oct. 22 X-Ray $122
Dec. 1   Visit to gastroenterologist $125
Dec. 4   Prescription $102

Emily met her $500 deductible in November. The following actual charges were incurred after she met her deductible:

Nov. 14 Visit to primary care physician $75
Nov. 14 Prescription $40
Dec. 15 Visit to primary care physician $75
Dec. 16 Visit to neurologist for migraine headaches $225
Dec. 16 MRI (other covered procedure) $1,200

Use their actual medical expenses to solve the following four problems:

1. Calculate the amount of medical expenses that Tyrone paid out-of-pocket (include his deductible and monthly premiums).
2. Calculate the amount of medical expenses that Emily paid out-of-pocket (include her deductible and monthly premiums).
3. Add together Tyrone and Emily's out-of-pocket medical expenses to find their total out-of-pocket medical expenses.
4. Divide their total out-of-pocket medical expenses by 12 to get their monthly budget figure for medical expenses.

Software Directions

You may utilize a spreadsheet program to organize Tyrone and Emily's expenses. Here is how to prepare a budget sheet using a spreadsheet program.

1. Start your spreadsheet software program.
2. Select **File** and **New** to begin a new workbook.
3. Begin by entering each column title in the top row. **One column for both Tyrone and Emily.** Add a third column for a description of each entry.
4. Select an entire column by clicking the column letter noted in gray and move the mouse to the column edge until a crosshatch appears. Pressing and holding the left mouse button, adjust the column width to your desired specifications, or double-click the button on the edge of the column to automatically fit each column.
5. For each row, enter actual medical expenses for last year into the designated column for each individual.
6. After entering all applicable medical expenses for both Tyrone and Emily, total each column by double clicking the summation symbol (Σ).
7. Perform the same steps for totaling both **Tyrone and Emily's total medical expenditures.**
8. Beneath the cell total for both Tyrone and Emily, **input** the numeral **12**.
9. To compute the monthly average for total expenditures, **divide** the cell "**total for both Tyrone and Emily**" by the cell containing the numeral 12 (e.g., = A1/A2).

————Activity 4————

Jim and Lauren Ritzi received a gift from Jim's father of $5,000. They want to use this money to help pay for a boat they're hoping to buy next year. For now, they want to put the money in a safe account but would like to earn as much interest as possible. Their bank has given them three accounts from which to choose. All three accounts are insured for up to $100,000.

Option 1: A savings account paying 4 percent simple interest, no minimum balance.

Option 2: A money market account paying 5 percent simple interest, $1,000 minimum balance.

Option 3: One year CD paying 6 percent simple interest with the loss of all interest for early withdrawal.

Jim and Lauren plan on keeping the money in whichever account they select for one year unless an unexpected expense arises.

REQUIRED: Calculate the amount of interest for each choice. Which would you suggest they choose and why?

COMPREHENSIVE PROBLEM

This comprehensive problem has two parts.

Part 1

In this unit you were introduced to Ann and Rick Miller. As you know, Ann and Rick attended a financial planning course to help them manage their personal finances. On the last night of the course the instructor asked each couple to set some new financial goals based on what they had learned in the course. These are the Miller's goals:

- Reduce high-interest credit card debt and limit credit card spending.
- Find savings accounts that pay higher interest rates or offer free services like no-fee checking accounts or low-rate loans.
- Use a monthly budget to keep track of their spending and help monitor their financial goals.
- Buy a small camper that can be towed on the back of Rick's truck for weekend getaways and vacations.

Ann and Rick's joint checking account is at First Federal of Ormond Beach. First Federal doesn't pay interest on this account and charges a $10 a month fee if the balance in the account drops below $1,000 at any time during the month. Ann and Rick opened their account at First Federal of Ormond Beach because it was close to their house. Ann's savings account is at Volusia Federal Credit Union, and Rick's savings account is at Heritage Bank. Ann called Volusia Federal Credit Union and Heritage Bank to get information on both checking and savings accounts. The information follows:

Volusia Federal Credit Union checking accounts
Minimum balance: $10
Monthly service fee: none
Check order fee: $8 per order; free checks if customer has savings account or money market account with balance over $1,000.
ATM withdrawal fee: none

Heritage Bank checking accounts
Minimum balance: none
Monthly service fee: $7.50—waived if customer has a savings account with a balance over $5,000.
ATM withdrawal fee: none

Volusia Federal Credit Union savings accounts
Minimum balance: $50
Interest rate: $2\frac{1}{2}$ percent

Volusia Federal Credit Union money market accounts
Minimum balance: $1,000
Interest rate: 4 percent

Heritage Bank savings accounts
Minimum balance: $100
Interest rate: 3 percent

Heritage Bank money market accounts
Minimum balance: $2,500
Interest rate: 4 percent

Remember that Rick has three credit cards with ongoing monthly balances. These cards include Sears (at 1.75 percent per month), Visa (at 1.5 percent per month) and Dillards (at 1 percent per month). These three businesses use the unpaid balance method to calculate the finance charge.

The Millers want to use any money in excess of $2,500 in their savings to reduce their credit card debt. Then they want to budget at least $300 a month toward eliminating their remaining credit card debt.

REQUIRED:

1. Calculate the monthly finance charge on each of the Millers' credit cards. Assume the balances on the Sears, Dillards, and Visa credit cards are the same as the balances appearing on their personal balance sheet in Table 2.1.
2. Calculate how much money (excess of $2,500) can be withdrawn from savings to reduce the most expensive credit cards or portions of credit cards. What are the balances left on each credit card?
3. Decide where the Millers should deposit their checking account and savings account money.
4. Prepare a new personal balance sheet for the Millers reflecting changes in savings. Refer to Table 2.1 in this unit for their personal balance sheet before the changes. Remove FORM 15 on page 81 to complete the personal balance sheet.

Note: You may utilize spreadsheet directions to prepare step four. Please refer back to the set of directions on how to prepare a personal balance sheet in Unit 1, Activity 1.

Part 2

The Millers' take home pay is $4,525 a month. Rent is $850, and they spend about $250 a month on utilities. Ann estimates that their monthly food expense is $600 because they eat out a lot. They spend an additional $400 a month on entertainment and vacations. Both agreed that they spend too much on clothes so they are budgeting $200 a month on clothing. Their monthly car insurance premiums total $105 and they spend around $180 on gas. Their cable television bill is $52 a month. Last year their out-of-pocket medical expenses averaged $190 a month, including premiums and medical expenses not covered by their HMO. Rick decided to get disability insurance and the premium for the policy is $38 a month. They give $100 a month to charity and pay $500 for their education expenses. They agreed to budget $250 for savings and $200 for miscellaneous expenses.

REQUIRED: Prepare a monthly budget for Ann and Rick. Don't forget they agreed to pay $300 a month on their credit cards and to pay $310 a month on Rick's truck loan. Remove FORM 16 page 83 to use in completing the monthly budget.

Software Directions

You may prepare this activity with personalized financial software. Follow these steps to prepare a monthly budget in Microsoft Money.
1. At the top of the screen, click **Planner**.
2. Under the headline, "tasks you do most often" select **create a budget**.
3. On the left-hand side of the screen, click **Income**.
4. Click **add category**… in the bottom left corner.
5. Select the category **other income**. Add a new subcategory called **expense reimbursement**.
6. **Finish** to add the new category to the budget.
7. Utilize the **Wages and Salary: Net Pay** for entering their monthly income.
8. On the left-hand side of the screen, click **Expenses**.
9. Eliminate all expense accounts except for ones needed.
10. Enter the total monthly expense amounts for each corresponding category.

11. On the left-hand side of the screen, select **monthly summary** to review the monthly budget for the Millers.

Software Directions

Follow these steps to prepare a monthly budget in Quicken:
1. At the top of the screen, click **Planning** and then **Budgeting**.
2. Under the left-hand side of the screen, select **categories** and checkmark all the individual categories necessary for preparing the budget for the Millers and click on **OK**.
3. Within the budgeting worksheet, select the **options** menu on the right-hand side of the screen.
4. Under the options menu click **Display Months**.
5. Select the month to input the budget data.
6. Click the category cell and enter the budgeted amount in the corresponding field. Note that all positive amounts appear in black and negative amounts in red.
7. After entering the entire budget, return to your financing home page. Your budget will be saved automatically.

Critical Thinking   The Millers have been looking at used campers and estimate the type they want costs $5,000. They decided to wait until they have the money saved and pay cash for the camper. At their present rate of saving, how long will it take them to save the $5,000 (disregard interest)? How can they trim their expenses so they can buy the camper soon?

_____

_____

_____

_____

_____

_____

_____

_____

_____

_____

_____

The *Expanding* Family

After completing this unit, you will be able to:

- Compare and contrast different types of home loans.

- Calculate monthly mortgage payments using a principal and interest table.

- Calculate the total amount of interest paid for the term of a home loan.

- Know how property taxes and residential insurance affect mortgage payments.

- Calculate mortgage discount points.

- Define basic terminology related to estate planning.

There is never a dull moment in the Allendes' household. Ruth and Lou Allendes juggle their full-time jobs with spending quality time with their two kids—Isabel and Miguel—and Ruth's mother, Maria, who moved in with the family a few years after her husband died. Ruth and Lou had decided after the death of Ruth's father that Maria was too far away from them. So they decided to move Maria from Austin, Tex., to McAllen, Tex. Initially, Maria was unsure about moving in because she didn't want to impose on their family, but she changed her mind because she really wanted to spend more time with her grandchildren, whom she absolutely adores.

Maria has had a chance to see Isabel in action in her school play, as well as Miguel kick the winning goals during soccer games. While the Allendes' work during the day, Maria involves herself in a variety of community volunteer organizations. Every day she picks up the kids from school or club practice.

Both Ruth and Lou work overtime since they are saving up to buy a house. At Maria's request, they are trying to find a home where Maria can have her own living quarters and still provide daily help with the kids. Ruth and Lou have $15,000 in a five-year CD that matures this month and $10,000 in a money market account that is available at any time. They also have $3,200 in a savings account for emergencies. Table 3.1 shows a combined personal balance sheet for Ruth and Lou.

Every weekend they glance through the Sunday newspaper's classified section to scout out the new houses for sale. Each Sunday they get more and more excited for the day when they can find the "right" home.

The "Big" Purchase

A home is the most expensive purchase most people will make in their lifetime. The majority of homebuyers don't have enough money saved so they make a down payment and take out a loan, or **mortgage**, on a home. There are three common ways to borrow money to buy a home: Federal Housing Administration (FHA), Veterans Affairs (VA), and conventional.

The **Federal Housing Administration (FHA)** is a government agency that insures or guarantees mortgages made by approved lenders. Under this type of loan, the borrower can put three percent or less down, and there are different plans from

Table 3.1

RUTH AND LOU ALLENDES' PERSONAL BALANCE SHEET
PREPARED SEPTEMBER 30, 20--

ASSETS		
Checking Account	$ 822	
Savings	3,200	
Money Market	10,000	
CD	15,000	
Cars	24,000	
Other Assets	10,000	
Total Assets		**$63,022**
LIABILITIES		
MasterCard	$ 1,450	
Car Loan	8,200	
Total Liabilities		$9,650
NET WORTH		53,372
Total Liabilities and Net Worth		**$63,022**

Do the Allendes have enough money in their checking account to completely pay off their MasterCard?
Answer: No, they only have $822 in their checking account.

which to select regarding monthly payments. Not all borrowers or homes qualify for FHA financing because there is a maximum loan amount depending on the area in which the home is located.

If you're a veteran, you're eligible for the **Veterans Affairs (VA) mortgage**, which is another way to borrow money. This type of loan is guaranteed by the Veterans Administration and usually

Keywords

Mortgage – loan on a home.
Federal Housing Administration (FHA) – government agency that insures or guarantees mortgages made by approved lenders.
Veterans Affairs (VA) mortgage – type of loan guaranteed by the Veterans Administration.

requires no down payment. Interest rates for VA loans are usually about the same as FHA loans.

The third way to borrow money for a home is through conventional financing. **Conventional loans** are made by private lenders and are not insured by the government. They usually have a higher interest rate than FHA or VA loans. Conventional loans typically require a down payment of 20 percent unless the borrower agrees to buy private mortgage insurance. **Private mortgage insurance (PMI)** protects the lender if the borrower stops paying the loan.

When you shop for a home loan you will have the option of selecting a fixed-rate mortgage or an adjustable-rate mortgage. A **fixed-rate mortgage** locks you into a specific interest rate for the term of the loan, typically 15 or 30 years. Your payment is the same each month.

With an **adjustable-rate mortgage (ARM)** the interest rate changes periodically, usually at least once a year. The rate is tied to an index such as the Treasury Bill Index or the Federal Home Loan Bank's interest rate. Lenders usually take the given index rate and add several points to that rate to determine your interest rate each year. The rate on ARMs is usually reduced for the first year of the loan to attract borrowers. If you finance your home with an adjustable rate mortgage, it's important to find out what index the lender uses and what your maximum rate of interest would be if the index increases. During the 1990s ARMs were a good choice for a home-buyer because interest rates remained low throughout that decade.

When you decide how long to finance your home, you should ask yourself these questions: How much can I afford for monthly payments?

How much money (including interest) could I spend for this home? Table 3.2 compares a 15-year fixed-rate mortgage with a 30-year fixed-rate mortgage. It should give you an idea of how much money you can save in the long run by financing your home for a shorter period of time. However, financing your home for a longer period of time reduces your monthly payment. You can see the amount saved on the 15-year loan is significant ($164,240 − $72,080 = $92,160).

It's fairly simple to find the monthly payment for 15- and 30-year mortgages at various rates. Just use the monthly principal and interest table shown in Table 3.3. This table uses different multipliers, called factors, to make it possible for you to quickly calculate your monthly payment. To use the monthly principal and interest table follow these steps.

1. Divide the amount of the loan by 1,000.
2. Locate the interest rate in the left-hand column and the number of years (15 or 30).
3. Find the factor at the point where the interest and years intersect.
4. Multiply the quotient you calculated in step one by the factor you found in step two. This is your monthly payment.

Table 3.3

MONTHLY PRINCIPAL AND INTEREST TABLE

Interest Rate	15-Year	30-Year
6%	8.44	6.00
6½%	8.72	6.33
7%	8.99	6.66
7½%	9.28	7.00
8%	9.56	7.34
8½%	9.85	7.69
9%	10.15	8.05
9½%	10.45	8.41

Table 3.2

TABLE COMPARING A 15-YEAR FIXED-RATE MORTGAGE WITH A 30-YEAR FIXED-RATE MORTGAGE

	15-Year	30-Year
Amount of loan	$100,000	$100,000
Interest rate	8%	8%
Monthly payment	$956	$734
Total interest paid on loan	$72,080	$164,240

Here is an example of how to use the monthly principal and interest table. Suppose the Allendeses bought a home that cost $87,500—putting 20 percent down and financing the balance for 15 years at six and a half percent. The amount of their loan would be $70,000 ($87,500 − $87,500 × 20%).

The following demonstrates the mathematical steps taken:

Step 1 Divide the amount of the loan by 1,000. ($70,000 ÷ 1,000 = $70)

Step 2 Find the factor on the table. The factor is 8.72

Step 3 Multiply the amount calculated in step one by the factor found in step two. $70 × 8.72 = $610.40

This is the amount ($610.40) of your monthly payment.

After they find the amount of their monthly payment they can calculate the total amount of interest they will pay during the entire loan period. This can be done in two steps:

Step 1 Multiply your monthly payment by the number of months in the loan.

Step 2 Subtract the amount of your loan from the amount you got in step one.

In the above example, the Allendes' monthly payment was $610.40 with 180 months in the loan ($610.40 × 180 = $109,872 is the total payments for the life of the loan). To find how much of this is interest, subtract the amount of the loan from this number: $109,872 − $70,000 = $39,872.

THE "OTHER" FEES

Buying a home also includes more calculations on top of the mortgage payments in terms of principal and interest. Actually, most mortgage payments include taxes and insurance in addition to principal and interest. Each month the borrower is expected to include one-twelfth of the estimated property tax and residential insurance cost as part of the mortgage payment.

Property tax is the amount you pay to the local government based on the value of your home. Taxes from property are used to support the school system, non-profit hospitals, and local governments. The value of property for tax purposes is called **assessed value**. To calculate property tax, multiply the assessed value of the property by the tax rate. For example, if the assessed value of the Allendes' new home is $150,000 and the tax rate is three percent, then the annual property tax would be $4,500 ($150,000 × .03). The portion of this tax paid each month as part of their mortgage payment is $375 ($4,500 ÷ 12). Assessed values and property tax rates vary. For example, in Daytona Beach, Florida, homes are assessed at their fair market value, and the local tax rate is two and a half percent. In Port Henry, New York, homes are assessed at 80 percent of their fair market value, but the tax rate is five percent.

Residential insurance, also referred to as homeowner's insurance, covers your home, personal property, and legal liability if someone is injured on your property. As with medical insurance, residential insurance has premiums and deductibles.

When you buy homeowner's insurance it's important to select a policy that pays for replacement of the insurables. This protects you against inflation. For example, if you buy a house for $90,000 and it is destroyed five years later, the house might cost $100,000 to replace. Your insurance should pay $100,000 if you have replacement value insurance. If your annual residential insurance is $660, each month you include $55 as part of your monthly mortgage payment ($660 ÷ 12).

When lenders receive the tax and property portion of your mortgage payment, they are required to hold the money in an **escrow account**, a special savings account, until the tax and insurance expenses are due. Then the lenders pay the tax and insurance payments directly to the local government and insurance company. When you are budgeting for a home payment it's important to remember to include taxes and insurance as part of each monthly payment.

Keywords

Conventional loan – made by private lenders and not insured by the government.

Private mortgage insurance (PMI) – protects the lender if the borrower stops paying the loan.

Fixed-rate mortgage – locks in a specific interest rate for the term of the mortgage, typically 15 or 30 years.

Adjustable-rate mortgage (ARM) – the interest rate changes periodically, usually at least once a year.

Property tax – the amount you pay to the local government based on the value of your home.

Assessed value – the value of your property for tax purposes.

Residential insurance – covers your home, personal property, and legal liability if someone is injured on your property.

Escrow account – a special savings account in which the lender deposits your monthly insurance and tax payments until they come due.

THE LAST ITEMS TO CONSIDER WHEN BUYING A HOME

In addition to the actual monthly mortgage payment, there are other costs associated with buying a home. These costs come before and at the time you buy the home. The **up-front fees** are costs that you pay before you buy the home, and these vary widely from lender to lender. The two most common up-front fees are for your credit report and an appraisal. Credit reports were discussed in Unit 2. An **appraisal** is an independent opinion of how much the property is worth. There are licensed appraisers in every geographical area.

Closing costs are expenses you pay at the time you sign the final papers connected with buying your home. The **closing statement** is a prepared document that shows the portion of the closing costs that the buyer and the seller pay. Some common closing costs for the buyer are title searches, title insurance, attorney fees, recording fees, and prorated taxes.

Another closing cost for the buyer that is important to understand are mortgage discount points. A **mortgage discount point** is one percent of the amount of the loan. Points are charged by the lender to increase the yield on a mortgage without increasing the interest rate. For example, if you borrow $150,000 to buy a home and the loan includes two and a half points, you would have to come up with $3,750 ($150,000 × .025) at closing to cover the points. This amount is in addition to your other closing costs.

The Allendes' Estate

An estate is everything you own including your home, car, money, and other property. You should always have a plan in effect to make sure the appropriate people inherit your estate. There are two main things that can be completed to ensure that an owner's property passes to the right people upon the owner's death. The first is to set up ownership of the property so that it automatically passes to the other person. For example, suppose Ruth's mother Maria has $50,000 in a savings account that she wants to go to Ruth. Maria could add Ruth's name to the account as a joint tenant with right of survivorship. A **joint tenant with rights of survivorship** stipulates that if one of the owners dies, the property goes directly to the surviving owner. The risk involved with this type of ownership is that, in the case of a bank account, one owner can withdraw money without permission of the other.

The second way to insure the proper handling of your estate is to prepare a will. A **will** is a legal document that transfers your property to your named beneficiaries after you die. A lawyer should prepare this document since each state has different laws regarding inherited property and estates. If you die without a will, your property is distributed according to the laws of your state. **Intestate** means dying without a will. The property that is transferred by your will is subject to probate. **Probate** is the legal process of verifying your will through the courts.

When you have children under the age of 18, it is important that you make plans for their care and upbringing if both you and your spouse die. An attorney can set up a **guardianship agreement** that names specific people to care for your children. These are good preventive measures to take on a serious subject.

Keywords

Up-front fees – costs of buying a home that you pay before you buy the home.

Appraisal – independent opinion of how much your property is worth.

Closing statement – shows costs of both the buyer and seller that must be settled before the buyer assumes ownership of the home.

Mortgage discount point – one percent of the amount of the mortgage loan. Used by lenders to increase the yield on a mortgage without actually raising the interest rate.

Joint tenant with rights of survivorship – form of ownership where property passes directly to the surviving owner if the other owner dies.

Will – legal document that transfers property to named beneficiaries.

Intestate – dying without a will.

Probate – legal process of verifying your will through the courts.

Guardianship agreement – legal agreement that names specific people to care for your minor children.

Student Activities

INSTRUCTIONS: This section is designed for you to practice the concepts introduced in this unit. While completing the Student Activities, refer back to the unit text if you need help calculating mortgage payments, interest on a home loan, or mortgage discount points. Additionally, these activities may be completed by two methods: manually or automatically. The activities that merit automation include software directions.

You may use the Answer Sheet on pages 85 and 86 for activities not requiring FORMS. Remove the Answer Sheet before beginning the following activities and place it in your IN FILE. Once you have completed the activities place the Answer Sheet in the OUT FILE. Activities requiring FORMS include the page numbers of the FORMS and are filed appropriately in either the IN FILE or OUT FILE.

Activity 1

Barbara Yuma is buying a new home. The price of the home is $105,000, and she is putting down 20 percent in cash and borrowing the balance.

REQUIRED:

1. Find the amount of the loan.
2. Find the amount of Yuma's monthly payment (principal and interest) if she finances the home for 30 years at eight percent.
3. Calculate how much interest Yuma will pay over the life of the loan.

Software Directions

How to calculate Yuma's expenses in Microsoft Money:

1. Start by picking a task. Click on **House Center** from the **Go** menu at the top of the screen.
2. Click **calculate the cost of a loan**.
3. Select **Loan Terms** to calculate the amount of the loan.
4. Choose option 1 to calculate **Principal and Interest** for step one.
5. The payment frequency for the terms of the loan is monthly, and the length of the loan is 30 years.
6. Principal and interest should be left blank, as the Money program will automatically complete this amount.
7. Input the loan amount computed from step one ($105,000 × .80).
8. The starting interest rate is 8 percent, and there is no balloon payment.
9. Finally, click the **Calculate** button on the bottom to determine the principal and interest payment amount.
10. Total interest paid on the loan is automatically computed on the worksheet under the **Comparison** tab on the **Loan Planner Worksheet**.

How to calculate steps one and two in this activity using Quicken:

1. Go to **Household**, and click on **Loans**.
2. Click on the **Next** tab.
3. Click **Borrow money**, and click **Next**.
4. Select **New account**—label it "New Home loan." Click "no" on payments made.
5. Enter the date the loan was created, which will be today's date.
6. Enter the original amount borrowed found in step one ($84,000.).
7. Click "no" balloon payment.
8. Choose a 30-year loan.
9. Click **standard monthly period** and make sure the compounding period is monthly.
10. The date of the first payment is the next month.
11. Click **Don't know the amount of the first payment**.
12. Input eight percent as the interest rate, and click **Next**.
13. Under the **Summary** menu, check that loan information input is correct, and click **Next**.
14. Click **Done** to allow Quicken to calculate the next principle and interest payment.

To calculate step three of this activity in Quicken, the total interest is automatically calculated on the Payment Graph. Hover the cursor and click on the chart for the interest at any point in time.

————Activity 2————

Eva and Barry Kaufman are buying their first house. They found a new house in a nice neighborhood for $78,000. Barry found two lenders willing to finance the house with only five percent down. Major Bank & Trust offered them a 15-year, eight and a half percent mortgage; First National Bank offered them a 30-year, nine percent mortgage.

REQUIRED:

1. Find the amount of the Kaufmans' loan.
2. Find the monthly payment for each option.
3. Find the total amount of interest paid on each option.

Software Directions

Consult the software directions for Activity 1 to calculate these answers.

Critical Thinking   What are some of the considerations that the Kaufmans should think about before deciding which option to select?

_____

_____

_____

_____

_____

_____

_____

_____

_____

_____

_____

_____

————Activity 3————

Lincoln Properties, Inc., recently purchased several pieces of land. The assessed value of each piece is as follows:

Division Road	$230,000
West & Center	80,000
Fifth Street	180,000
Nebraska Avenue	76,000
Milton Drive	55,000

REQUIRED: If the property tax rate is three and a half percent of the assessed value, find the property tax on each piece of land.

Critical Thinking   Which is more important in relation to property tax—the assessed value or the tax rate?

_____

_____

_____

_____

_____

_____

_____

_____

_____

_____

————Activity 4————

Louise and Denton Bell bought a home for $120,000. They put down 10 percent and financed the balance for 30 years at eight and a half percent. The annual property tax on their home is three percent of its assessed value of $100,000, and their residential insurance is $720 a year.

REQUIRED: What is their monthly payment (include principal, interest, taxes, and insurance)?

Software Directions

Consult the software directions for Activity 1 to calculate these answers.

COMPREHENSIVE PROBLEM

Ruth and Lou Allendes have moved into a new home. Since Ruth was just promoted at the IRS, they thought it would be a good time to prepare a monthly budget, which includes both Ruth's new take-home pay of $2,910 and their increase in housing expenses. Lou earns $2,340 from Safety Home Services as an electrician. They have two cars—the BMW is paid off but the Taurus has 25 monthly payments left of $337. They spend approximately $130 a month on gas and another $50 on other car expenses. They have one credit card that they use to pay various expenses. Their home mortgage payment, including taxes and insurance, is $1,243. They spend around $500 a month on food, $700 on entertainment (which includes $240 for a family country club membership and $160 to a finance company toward their new entertainment center), and $250 on health care. Their utilities run around $350 a month, and they contribute $200 a month to their church. The Allendeses also send Lou's sister, Olivia, $150 a month to help pay for her college expenses. They budget $300 a month for clothes, $500 for savings, and the rest for miscellaneous expenses. Each month the Allendes write one check for the total amount for set-asides ($300). They deposit the money in their money market deposit account (MMDA) at Security Savings and Loan. The money earns interest and is available to meet their periodic fixed expenses. Table 3.4 is a table of set-asides for Ruth and Lou Allendes.

REQUIRED: Record all checking account transactions for the month in the Allendes' check register on page 125 and the financial record sheet, FORM 17 on page 87.

The Allendeses don't use a cash record sheet. However, they use a notepad on which major cash expenditures are recorded during the month and later listed on the financial record sheet.

Table 3.4

THE ALLENDES' SET-ASIDES

Item	Amount Set-Aside	Amount Needed	Paid
Auto Insurance	$100	$600	Semi-Annually (January & July)
Life Insurance			
Ruth	$40	$480	Annually (January)
Lou	$60	$720	Annually (January)
Home Maintenance	$100	$1,800 Goal	As Needed
TOTAL	**$300**		

How much money do the Allendeses set aside together for life insurance?
Answer: $100.00.

From this point in this activity, you will not write checks or make deposits. You will record these items directly into the check register, as if they were completed. Information for entries in the financial record sheet is then secured from the check register (See Table 3.5-3.9). After recording the following transactions in the check register and financial record sheet, use the following information to prepare Ruth and Lou Allendes' monthly budget (refer to FORM 18 on page 89).

Table 3.5

EXAMPLE OF SET-ASIDES IN THE CHECK REGISTER

Check No.	Date	Description		Payments	✓	Deposit	Balance
							4,612.00
107	8-4	Superior Savings		350.00			
		Auto Insurance	80.00				
		Life Insurance	120.00				
		Home Maintenance	150.00				

Table 3.6

EXAMPLE OF SET-ASIDES IN THE FINANCIAL RECORD SHEET, August 20--

Date	Chk.	Description	Receipts	Withdrawals	Payments	Clothing	Entertainment	Food	Health Care	Housing	Transportation	Miscellaneous	Savings/Investments
8-4	107	Superior Savings			350.00								
		Auto Insurance									80.00		
		Life Insurance											120.00
		Home Maintenance								150.00			

Table 3.7

EXAMPLE OF CREDIT CARD ENTRY IN THE CHECK REGISTER

Check No.	Date	Description		Payments	✓	Deposit	Balance 4,380.00
110	3-2	Fidelity Credit		736.62			3,643.38
		Clothing	218.12				
		Food	432.00				
		Entertainment	86.50				

Table 3.8

EXAMPLE OF CREDIT CARD ENTRY IN THE FINANCIAL RECORD SHEET, March 20--

Date	Chk.	Description	Receipts	With-drawals	Payments	Clothing	Enter-tainment	Food	Health Care	Housing	Trans-portation	Miscel-laneous	Savings/Investments
11-9	110	Fidelity Credit			736.62								
		Clothing				218.12							
		Food						432.00					
		Entertainment					86.50						

April 1 Lou deposited his monthly paycheck for $2,340.00 to open the account.

April 4 Ruth bought groceries at Price-Cutters (refer to FORM 19 page 91). Wrote check No. 101.

April 5 Lou sent his monthly car payment to Marathon Credit Union (refer to FORM 20 on page 91). Wrote check No. 102.

April 5 Lou withdrew $200.00 from an ATM.

April 6 Ruth deposited her monthly paycheck for $2,910.

April 8 Lou received his telephone bill from Eastern Bell (refer to FORM 21 on page 91). Wrote check No. 103.

April 9 Ruth paid the monthly set-asides to Security Savings and Loan. Wrote check No. 104 in the amount of $300.00 for the monthly set-asides. See Table 3.4 to determine how much is allocated for each of the monthly set-asides. Tables 3.5 and 3.6 show examples of how set-asides are handled in the check register and the financial record sheet, respectively.

April 10 Wrote check No. 105 for $636.32 to Hanson Credit, Inc., for total amount charged on the credit card last month. Charges included gas purchases of $121.16; clothing from JCPenny for $212; and Smart Groceries, Inc., $303.16. Tables 3.7 and 3.8 show how a similar entry is made in the check register and financial record sheet, respectively. Also wrote check No. 106 for $240 to Green Acres Country Club and check No. 107 for $160 for the entertainment center to Brown Finance Company.

April 12 Ruth withdrew $200 from an ATM.

April 19 Lou received the electric bill from Premium Power Company (refer to FORM 22 on page 93). Wrote check No. 108.

April 20 Lou bought groceries at Price-Cutters. Wrote check No. 109 for $78.16.

Table 3.9

EXAMPLE OF CASH PAYMENTS IN THE FINANCIAL RECORD SHEET, July 20--

Date	Chk.	Description	Receipts	With-drawals	Payments	Clothing	Enter-tainment	Food	Health Care	Housing	Trans-portation	Miscel-laneous	Savings/Investments
7-31	115	Cash Payments			120.00		40.00	60.00				20.00	

April 22 Lou withdrew $200 from an ATM.

April 26 Lou received his monthly cable bill from TCI Cable Company. Wrote check No. 110 for $57.25.

April 30 Ruth paid the monthly home mortgage to Home Mortgage, Inc. Wrote check No. 111 for $1,243.

April 30 Lou withdrew $200 from an ATM.

April 30 The Allendeses had $140 left from the $800 ATM withdrawals. The cash payments of $660 ($800 − $140) during April were spent on entertainment ($200), health care ($180), and miscellaneous ($280). Table 3.9 shows how an entry is made in the financial record sheet for cash payments.

Software Directions

Input data into an electronic register in one of the personal finance software programs or spreadsheet programs. Insert data corresponding to the account register. See software directions for Unit 1 on the bank reconciliation preparation and daily activity recording exercises as examples.

The *Head* of the Household With Child

After completing this unit, you will be able to:

- Describe the characteristics of selected tax sheltered retirement plans.

- Discuss factors in choosing an investment.

- Read a stock quotation table.

- Calculate price-earnings ratios.

- Define mutual funds.

- Read a bond quotation table.

L ucy Choi didn't move with her 12-year-old daughter Jessica from Boston to Brooklyn because of a career move. After the sudden death of Daniel Choi, husband and father, they made the tough decision to move to Brooklyn to be closer to Lucy's extended family.

They lived with her parents until Lucy found a two-bedroom apartment and a job. She landed a job as a paralegal for a prestigious law firm, which paid her well enough to send Jessica to a private school. Jessica immediately made friends at her new school by becoming an active participant in several school clubs like debate, student government, tennis, and basketball.

Lucy and Jessica usually got home about the same time every night and then made dinner together. They ate dinner in front of the television, watching their favorite sitcoms. After dinner Lucy usually read a book or painted while Jessica finished her homework. On the weekends they liked to go shopping or take long walks in Central Park while snacking on gelato.

Lucy's Transition Issues

Lucy was left with $250,000 after Daniel died. Daniel's employer offered a benevolent fund to assist with Jessica's tuition. After all the bills were paid Lucy had $210,000 left to invest. She set up an appointment with a financial adviser and took Jessica with her on their first visit. A **financial planner** helps people manage their money through tax and estate planning, pension plans, and investment strategies for a fee. The first thing the financial planner did was to prepare a personal balance sheet for Lucy. Table 4.1 shows Lucy's personal balance sheet.

Before investing any of Lucy's money for the long term, the financial planner asked Lucy to list her financial goals. She wanted to
- Set aside enough money for Jessica's college education.
- Purchase a condominium.
- Have enough money each year for them to take a two-week vacation.

Then the financial planner suggested Lucy prepare a monthly budget since both monthly income and monthly expenses had changed since they moved. Table 4.2 shows their monthly budget.

RETIREMENT PLAN

Lucy contributes pre-tax dollars to her retirement plan. She doesn't have to pay taxes on this money until she retires. This type of retirement savings is called a **401(k)**, which is named after the tax code it represents. Lucy can decide whether to

Table 4.1

LUCY CHOI
PERSONAL BALANCE SHEET
OCTOBER 31, 20--

ASSETS

Checking Account	$ 2,300	
Savings	210,000	
Furniture	8,000	
Car	17,000	
Other Assets	4,000	
Total Assets		$241,300

LIABILITIES	$ 0
NET WORTH	241,300
Total Liabilities and Net Worth	$241,000

What are Choi's liabilities?
Answer: None. Zero.

invest this money in stocks, bonds, or less risky investments like a CD or money market account. She can begin withdrawing from her investments without penalty at age 59½. Lucy can contribute up to $10,500 into her 401(k) each year.

Many employers match employee contributions as part of their benefit package. Thus, Lucy's employer offers another type of retirement plan into which contributions are made on her behalf. This plan is called a **Simplified Employee Pension (SEP)**. SEPs are funded by the employer but controlled by the employee. All the money

Keywords

Financial planner – helps people manage their money through tax and estate planning, pension plans, and investment strategies for a fee.
401K – type of tax sheltered retirement savings.
Simplified Employee Pension (SEP) – a retirement plan under which the employer contributes money into each employee's IRA.

Table 4.2

LUCY CHOI
MONTHLY BUDGET
PREPARED OCTOBER 31, 20--

INCOME
Take Home Pay	$4,500	
Interest From Savings	1,200	
Total Income		$5,700

EXPENSES
Rent	$1,750	
Food	800	
Travel & Entertainment	800	
Clothing	300	
Car Insurance	100	
Electric	200	
Gas	100	
Telephone	75	
Tuition	250	
Miscellaneous	250	
Total Expenses		4,625
Balance available for savings		$ 1,075

Which expense do you think Choi could decrease?

deposited into Lucy's SEP becomes her property as soon as her employer deposits it. The account that it is deposited into it is called an **Individual Retirement Account (IRA)**. IRAs may or may not be taxed depending on several factors.

GENERAL INVESTMENT FACTORS

A person's investments should be based on his or her goals. Individuals and families have different investment goals. Some want safety. Others prefer a large return as quickly as possible. Still others look for long-term growth. When choosing an investment, consider the following factors:

Safety – How safe will your money be? How comfortable are you with risk? Generally the safer the investment, the lower the rate of return. For example, U.S. Treasury bills or savings bonds most often have a lower return than common stock in a new technology company. Investors should consider whether they can afford the risk of losing the entire investment for the chance to earn a high return.

Liquidity – **Liquidity** refers to how quickly your investment can be converted to cash. Certain investments such as real estate or collectibles may take some time to sell.

Investment expenses – Sometimes you must pay a fee or commission when you buy or sell an investment. You may also be charged a penalty if you withdraw funds early.

Yield – The **yield** is the income you earn from your investment. What income can you reasonably expect from your investment? Some investments earn dividends or interest on a regular basis. Others increase in value over time.

Purchasing power – Will your investment shrink in purchasing power? Are you protected against loss in time of inflation (an increase in the cost of living)?

To meet your objectives, you should choose investments that combine these factors. Since no single investment has all the advantages, selecting different types of investments may offer the greatest benefit. The strengths of one investment will offset the weaknesses of another.

STOCKS

Corporations are formed and expanded with money known as **capital** that is raised by issuing shares of stock. When you buy stock in a corporation you are an investor and owner of that corporation. When you own stock you get a return on your investment in two ways: dividend and capital appreciation. A **dividend** is a distribution of the corporation's profits to its owners. **Capital appreciation** is when the selling price or value of the stock you own goes up. For example, you might buy 100 shares of McDonald's for $50 a share and it might be selling for $55 a share the following month. The stock has risen in value by $5 a share. The value of your stock has risen by $500 ($5 × 100 shares).

Before you invest in stock you need to know how to read the stock quotation tables that are found in the business section of most newspapers. Table 4.3 shows what the McDonald's stock quotation looks like in the business section of a newspaper. Under the stock quotation is an explanation of what each column means.

Before you select stocks as one of your investments, there are a few basic things that you should know about the stock market. The stock market tends to rise and fall in cycles. Many things contribute to these cycles including the economic environment and the political environment. During times when the Federal Reserve is putting

Table 4.3

EXAMPLE OF A STOCK QUOTATION TABLE

52-week Hi	52-week Lo	Stock	Sym	Div	Yld %	PE	Vol 100s	Hi	Lo	Close	Net Chg
66½	45¼	McDonald's	MCD	.33	.5	28	30,124	66	63½	65⅞	+ 3¹⁄₁₆

Column 1	(66½)	Highest selling price of the stock during the preceding 52 weeks ($66.50).
Column 2	(45¼)	Lowest selling price of the stock during the preceding 52 weeks ($45.25).
Column 3	(McDonald's)	Company name.
Column 4	(MCD)	Ticker symbol.
Column 5	(.33)	Last year's dividend ($.33).
Column 6	(.5)	Yield. Last year's dividend ÷ current price (.5%).
Column 7	(28)	Price earnings ratio. Current price ÷ earnings per share.
Column 8	(30,124)	Number of shares traded this day × 100 (3,012,400).
Column 9	(66)	Highest price the stock traded during this day ($66).
Column 10	(63½)	Lowest price the stock traded during this day ($63.50).
Column 11	(65⅞)	Last price the stock traded during this day ($65.875).
Column 12	(+ 3¹⁄₁₆)	Change between the closing price yesterday and this day (+$3.0625).

What does it mean if you say that McDonald's was up 3¹⁄₁₆ today?
Answer: The stock price closed at a price $3.0625 higher today than yesterday.

money into the economy, stocks tend to rise. Historically, economists have not been very successful in predicting which individual stocks will rise and fall, especially in the short run. That is why stocks are one of the more risky investments.

Price-earnings ratio

One common way many investors select which stocks to buy is by looking at the company's price-earnings ratio. The **price-earnings ratio (P-E ratio)** is the current price of a stock divided by the company's earnings per share. Some investors believe that stocks with low P-E ratios are undervalued and good to buy. However, you always run the risk that a company with a low P-E ratio means that investors are not optimistic about the stock. If Maytag's current price is $59.50 and the company's earnings per share is $3.50, the P-E ratio would be 17 ($59.50 ÷ $3.50).

Mutual funds

If selecting individual stocks for your portfolio seems overwhelming and too risky, you might want to invest in mutual funds. A **mutual fund** pools money from many investors and purchases stock in a number of companies. There are many types of mutual funds. Some specialize by the size of the company (e.g., large, medium, or small), while others specialize by the type of company such as real estate, oil, or high-tech. Investing in a mutual fund is one way to buy stocks and bonds yet spread your risk among many companies without having to invest too much money.

Bonds

A **bond** is a promise to repay borrowed money. Corporations can borrow money long term by issuing bonds. Bondholders have first claim on the assets of a corporation if the corporation goes out of business. Thus, investing in bonds is less risky than investing in stocks. The **face value** of a bond is the original amount of money borrowed by the company. After that the bond can be bought and sold on the open market just like stock. The sell-

Keywords

Individual Retirement Account (IRA) – an account under which certain individuals are allowed to deposit money for their retirement.

Liquidity – how quickly your investment can be converted to cash.

Yield – the income you earn from an investment.

Capital – money raised to form and expand corporations.

Dividend – distribution of a corporation's profit to its owners.

Capital appreciation – when the value of a stock goes up.

Price-earnings ratio – current price of a stock divided by the company's earnings per share.

Mutual fund – pools money from many investors and purchases stocks and bonds in a number of companies.

Bond – long-term debt of a corporation.

Face value – original amount borrowed on a bond.

Table 4.4

EXAMPLE OF A BOND QUOTATION TABLE

Bonds	Curr Yld	Vol	Close	Net Chg
Dole	6¾ 03	6½	100	103⅛	+¼

Column 1	Dole is the company name, 6¾ percent is the interest rate the bonds pay and 03 indicates that the bonds mature in 2003.
Column 2	The current yield on these bonds is 6½ percent.
Column 3	100, $1,000 bonds were sold on this day.
Column 4	The close price is the current price of the bonds in the market. 103⅛ indicates that the bond is selling at 103.125 percent of its face value of $1,000.

ing price of the bond will then be determined by market conditions at the time of the sale. Table 4.4 explains a bond quotation table.

Optional Tax Return

During January taxpayers receive their tax return form (FORM 1040A) from the **Internal Revenue Service (IRS)**. The IRS is the branch of the U.S. Treasury Department that is responsible for administering tax law. Employers are also required to send each employee a record of his or her prior year's earnings before the end of January. The prior year's earnings record is called a **W-2**, and it contains information taxpayers need in order to complete their tax return including the total taxable amount they earned and the amount of taxes withheld by their employer. In Student Activities you will have the opportunity to fill out an individual's tax return. This is good practice since everyone has to pay taxes each year.

Keywords

Internal Revenue Service (IRS) – the branch of the U.S. Treasury Department that is responsible for administering tax law.

W-2 – a statement of an employee's prior year's earnings.

Student Activities

This section is designed for you to practice the concepts introduced in this unit. In the Student Activities, refer back to this unit for important tables and how to read a stock quotation table and to calculate the P-E ratio.

You may use the Answer Sheet on pages 95 and 96 for activities not requiring FORMS. Remove the Answer Sheet before beginning the following activities and place it in your IN FILE. Once you have completed the activities place the Answer Sheet in the OUT FILE. Activities requiring FORMS include the page numbers of the FORMS and are filed appropriately in either the IN FILE or OUT FILE.

Activity 1

Jean Fortner is a married 52-year-old doctor. She owns 500 shares of Brown & Brown and 200 shares of Brunswick. The following stock quotations found in *The Wall Street Journal* include information on these two companies.

REQUIRED: Use Table 4.5 to answer the following questions:

1. What was the highest price at which Brown & Brown sold during the last 52 weeks?
2. How many shares of Brown & Brown traded on this day?
3. What is Brown & Brown's P-E ratio?
4. Approximately how much money did Fortner make on Brown & Brown stock between yesterday and today?

Table 4.5

52-week Hi	Lo	Stock	Sym	Div	Yld %	PE	Vol 100s	Hi	Lo	Close	Net Chg
50¹¹⁄₁₆	30¾	Brown & Brown	BRO	.52	1.0	24	133	50¹¹⁄₁₆	49¹³⁄₁₆	50¹¹⁄₁₆	+⅞
64⅛	41½	BrownFomm	BFA	1.24	2.3	17	27	54	54	54	-¼
21¾	8½	BrownShoe	BWS	.40	3.1	7	985	13	12⅝	13	+⅜
30	14¾	Brunswick	BC	.50	2.8	42	4057	18⅛	17³⁄₁₆	17⁹⁄₁₆	+⅞

5. What was the last price that Brunswick traded for this day?

6. If Fortner bought her 200 shares of Brunswick when it was at its lowest price during the past 52 weeks, how much did she pay?

7. What amount of total dividends would an investor have received last year with 1,000 shares of Brunswick?

8. If Fortner bought another 100 shares of Brunswick just as the market closed, how much did she pay?

Critical Thinking If Fortner continues to invest in only these two companies, what kind of risk is associated with this investment?

_____

_____

_____

_____

_____

_____

_____

_____

_____

_____

————Activity 2————

Below is a list of five stocks that Rudy Spears owns along with each stock's current price and earnings per share.

SYM	Current Price	E.P.S.
EFU	67½	$2.50
FMK	14	$1.75
HDL	12¼	$1.75
THX	20	$1.00
PXP	10½	$ .75

REQUIRED: Calculate the P-E ratio for each stock.

————Activity 3————

Antonio Rodriquez has 10, $1,000 Chase bonds and 20, $1,000 IBM bonds. The following bond quotations found in *The Wall Street Journal* include information on the bonds of these two companies.

Bonds	Curr Yld	Vol	Close	Net Chg
ChaseM 7½ 03	7.4	25	100⅞	-¼
Exxon 6 05	6.2	22	96¼	-⅜
IBM 7¼ 02	7.2	241	100⅜	+⅛

REQUIRED: Use the data above to answer the following questions:

1. Is the current yield higher or lower than the interest rate on the Chase bonds?
2. How many IBM bonds were sold on this day?
3. When will the Chase bonds mature?
4. Did the IBM bonds close higher or lower than yesterday?
5. How much annual interest in dollars will each one of Antonio's Chase bonds pay?

————Activity 4————

Kevin Lee, Lucy's 25-year-old brother, is a customer service representative for First Federal Bank of New York. Remove FORM 23 on pages 97 and 99 and fill out Kevin's 1040A—a tax form appropriate for his situation. Use Kevin's W-2 (see Table 4.6) and his 1040A to complete the following steps:

Step 1: Complete the Label section including name, address, and Social Security number. Use your own opinion to fill in the information for the Presidential Election Campaign Fund.

Step 2: Complete the Filing status section. Kevin is single.

Step 3: Complete the Exemptions section. As a taxpayer he is entitled to an exemption for himself, his spouse, and each person he may support who qualifies as his dependent. Kevin has no dependents but can claim himself.

Table 4.6

KEVIN LEE'S W-2 STATEMENT

a Control number			OMB No. 1545-0008			
b Employer's identification number			1 Wages, tips, other compensation		2 Federal income tax withheld	
59-4931199			34,110.00		4,896.00	
c Employer's name, address, and ZIP code			3 Social security wages		4 Social security tax withheld	
First Federal Bank of New York			34,110.00		2,114.82	
1001 Washington Street			5 Medicare wages and tips		6 Medicare tax withheld	
New York, NY 10004			34,110.00		494.60	
			7 Social security tips		8 Allocated tips	
d Employee's social security number			9 Advance EIC payment		10 Dependent care benefits	
265-43-5458						
e Employee's name, address, and ZIP code			11 Nonqualified plans		12 Benefits included in box 1	
Kevin Lee			13		14 Other	
201 Rollins Ave. Apt 201						
New York, NY 10004						

15 Statutory employee	Deceased	Pension plan	Legal rep.	Hshld. emp.	Subtotal	Deferred compensation

16 State	Employer's state I.D. no.	17 State wages, tips, etc.	18 State income tax	19 Locality name	20 Local wages, tips, etc.	21 Local income tax
NY	69-0610324	34,110.00	1,939.54	NY City	34,110.00	1,183.28

Form **W-2** Wage and Tax Statement 20--

Copy 1 For State, City, or Local Tax Department

Department of the Treasury – Internal Revenue Service

Table 4.7

Step 4: Complete the Income section. Record the total wages earned by Kevin on line 7, as shown on his W-2. Record the amount of his interest income ($220) on line 8a. Calculate Kevin's total income and enter it on line 15.

Step 5: Bring down the total income amount from line 15 to line 19 and to line 20 on the top of page two.

Step 6: Enter Kevin's standard deduction on line 22. A taxpayer's standard deduction depends on his or her filing status but can be adjusted if the taxpayer or spouse is 65 or over, blind, has unearned income, or is being claimed as a dependent by another taxpayer. Kevin does not qualify for any of these special adjustments.

Step 7: Find Kevin's taxable income. Subtract line 22 from line 20 and enter the total on line 23. Next, follow the instructions on line 24. Now, subtract line 24 from line 23 and place the difference on line 25.

Step 8: Part of a federal tax table is shown in Table 4.7. Use this table to find the amount of tax owed by Kevin. Enter the tax amount on line 26 and bring it down to line 35.

Step 9: Enter the amount of federal income tax

PART OF A FEDERAL TAX TABLE

If line 39 (taxable income) is		And your are—			
At least	But less than	Single	Married filing jointly	Married filing separately	Head of a house-hold
			Your tax is—		
27,000					
27,000	27,050	4,220	4,054	4,769	4,054
27,050	27,100	4,234	4,061	4,783	4,061
27,100	27,150	4,248	4,069	4,797	4,069
27,150	27,200	4,262	4,076	4,811	4,076
27,200	27,250	4,276	4,084	4,825	4,084
27,250	27,300	4,290	4,091	4,839	4,091
27,300	27,350	4,304	4,099	4,853	4,099
27,350	27,400	4,318	4,106	4,867	4,106
27,400	27,450	4,332	4,114	4,881	4,114
27,450	27,500	4,346	4,121	4,895	4,121
27,500	27,550	4,360	4,129	4,909	4,129
27,550	27,600	4,374	4,136	4,923	4,136
27,600	27,650	4,388	4,144	4,937	4,144
27,650	27,700	4,402	4,151	4,951	4,151
27,700	27,750	4,416	4,159	4,965	4,159
27,750	27,800	4,430	4,166	4,979	4,166
27,800	27,850	4,444	4,174	4,993	4,174
27,850	27,900	4,458	4,181	5,007	4,181
27,900	27,950	4,472	4,189	5,021	4,189
27,950	28,000	4,486	4,196	5,035	4,196

withheld from Kevin's pay on line 36 according to his W-2. Bring the amount on line 36 down to line 40.

Step 10: Follow the directions for lines 41 through 44 to find whether Kevin owes additional taxes or whether he is entitled to a refund. Write the amount on the appropriate line.

Step 11: Sign and date the tax return for Kevin. Use January 31 of the current year. Enter Kevin's occupation on the right side of the form on the appropriate line.

COMPREHENSIVE PROBLEM

After several meetings with her financial planner Lucy Choi contacted a real estate agent and they began looking for a two-bedroom condo. They finally found one close to Lucy's office and Jessica's school. Lucy paid $190,000 for the condo putting $90,000 down in cash and financing the balance of $100,000 for 15 years at seven and a half percent. Closing costs and other costs associated with the purchase of the new condo for Lucy were $5,000. The annual property tax on the new condo is $5,400 and the annual residential insurance is $2,400.

Lucy's new checking account balance is $1,800 and the estimated value of her furniture, car, and other assets have not changed since preparing her previous personal balance sheet. (See Table 4.1.)

Lucy doesn't pay rent after purchasing the condo and her estimated interest from savings is reduced to $400. Lucy's monthly take-home pay and all other estimated expenses, except those relating to the purchase of the condo, have not changed. (See Table 4.2.)

After Lucy closed on her condo, she put $30,000 in a money market trust fund for Jessica's education. This account pays eight percent compounded yearly. Lucy doesn't enter Jessica's trust fund account on her personal balance sheet.

REQUIRED:
1. How much money is left in Lucy's savings account after these transactions? (Refer to Table 4.1 for Lucy's original savings balance.)
2. What are Lucy's monthly mortgage (principal and interest) payments? (Refer to Unit 3, Table 3.3 for a monthly principal and interest table.)
3. How much will be in Jessica's money market trust fund account at the end of 5 years?
4. Remove FORM 24 on page 101 and prepare Lucy's new personal balance sheet, which should be dated December 31st.
5. Remove FORM 25 on page 103 and prepare Lucy's new monthly budget, which should also be dated December 31st.

Critical Thinking   What should Lucy do with the money left in her savings account?

_____
_____
_____
_____
_____
_____
_____
_____
_____
_____
_____
_____
_____
_____
_____
_____
_____
_____
_____
_____
_____
_____
_____
_____
_____
_____
_____
_____

The *Older* Married Couple

After completing this unit, you will be able to:

- Discuss the purpose of an investment club.

- Compare and contrast different types of bonds.

- Calculate the equivalent yield on a municipal bond.

- Describe the basics of Social Security.

- Compare the difference between defined contribution and defined benefit pension plans.

- Identify who qualifies for a Keogh.

Durango and Brooke Mendoza celebrated their 40th wedding anniversary at a gathering hosted by Winona, the oldest of their three daughters. The celebration was in Ridgeview, Ind., a small town not far from South Bend. All the Mendoza daughters and some of Brooke's extended family live in Ridgeview, where Durango and Brooke have lived for over 30 years.

During the anniversary party Durango announced he would be retiring from the Ridgeview Construction Company within the year. He has worked as the general manager for the company for nearly 15 years. He started with the company as a roofer 30 years ago and worked his way up to management.

Durango plans to help his wife with her small greeting card shop, which she has owned and operated for nearly 10 years. Prior to owning her own business, she worked as a secretary for Ridgeview Elementary School. They hope to keep the shop as long as they can.

The Mendozas continue to plan their retirement by setting goals and making sure their finances will be sufficient to reach them. They have invested in the stock market the last 10 years. Durango also has a company retirement plan and is eligible for Social Security this year. Brooke has her income from the card shop and plans to keep it until she is eligible for her school system pension, Social Security, and the retirement fund through the card shop.

The Mendozas prepared a personal balance sheet to monitor their spending and to make sure that their debts are all paid off prior to retirement. Table 5.1 shows their personal balance sheet.

The Mendoza's Personal Investments

You have learned that people select investments based upon their individual goals. People have different investment goals at different times in their lives. Many families have little extra to invest while their children are young since they aren't in their peak earning years. Unfortunately, some families get into the habit of not saving and it stays with them.

The Mendozas made sacrifices along the way to put some money in the stock market. They always bought used cars, bought most of their clothes on sale, and tried to pay off their credit cards each month. As a result, they now have $235,000 in the stock market, and their house and cars are paid off. Their main goal concerning their stock portfolio is to transfer the money into less risky investments, which will provide them with steady income to supplement their other sources of retirement income.

Table 5.1

DURANGO AND BROOKE MENDOZA PERSONAL BALANCE SHEET
SEPTEMBER 30, 20--

ASSETS		
Cash	$ 4,000	
Savings Account	8,000	
Stocks/Mutual Funds	235,000	
House	120,000	
Cars	16,000	
Other Assets	10,000	
Total Assets		$393,000
LIABILITIES		$ 0
NET WORTH		393,000
Total Liabilities and Net Worth		**$393,000**

During the last few years Brooke has belonged to an investment club. An **investment club** is a group of people that pool their money and invest in the stock market. Each member in Brooke's club contributes $100 a month and they share in the research necessary to pick the stocks in which they invest. Her share of the investment club's assets is $11,000 and is included as part of the stocks and mutual funds on the personal balance sheet. Brooke plans to stay in the investment club even after she retires since it's a social activity she enjoys. The club meets once a week at a different member's home.

Keyword

Investment club – group of people that pool their money and invest in the stock market.

Table 5.2

EQUIVALENT TAXABLE YIELD EXAMPLE
(28% Income Tax Bracket and 6% Municipal Bond Interest Rate)

$$\text{Equivalent Taxable Yield} = \text{Tax Exempt Yield (Rate of Municipal)} \times \frac{1}{100\% - \text{Tax Rate}}$$

$$= 6\% \times \frac{1}{100\% - 28\%}$$

$$= 6\% \times \frac{1}{72\%}$$

$$= .083 = 8.3\%$$

INVESTING IN BONDS

The Mendozas are considering moving most of their money out of stocks and putting it into bonds for greater safety and reliable income. There are many different kinds of bonds, but only some of which provide the safety and income that they need.

The safest of all bonds is the U.S. Treasury bond. The U.S. government guarantees **Treasury bonds**. The interest rate is usually low because you don't have a high risk when you invest in a Treasury bond. One advantage of Treasury bonds is that their income is free from state and local taxes.

Series EE savings bonds are also a very safe investment. **Series EE bonds** are issued by the U.S. government, mature in 12 years, and have interest rates based on Treasury note yields.

Interest on a Series EE bond is not paid until the bond is sold. There isn't any income tax to pay until that time, unless the holder of the bond prefers to pay the tax yearly.

Another type of bond is the government agency bond. **Government agency bonds**, including Government National Mortgage Association, Federal National Mortgage Association, and Federal Home Loan Mortgage Corporation, were created to help housing in this country grow. These agencies purchase high-quality mortgages from lenders and sell partial interests in these mortgage pools to investors. Unlike most bonds that pay interest semi-annually, these bonds pay interest monthly. They also pay the investor part of principal back each month. These bonds are very safe as investments.

Municipal bonds are not subject to federal income tax. Therefore, the higher the tax bracket

of an individual, the higher the after-tax yield on a municipal bond compared to a taxable bond. For example, if you are in the 28 percentile of a tax bracket, a 10 percent municipal bond's yield would be equivalent to a 13.89 percent taxable bond. If you were in the 31 percent tax bracket, the same 10 percent municipal bond's yield would be equivalent to a 14.49 percent taxable bond. It's important to compare your after-tax yield on a municipal bond with other taxable investments before you decide which is right for you.

To find the equivalent yield on a municipal bond use the following formula:

$$\text{Equivalent Taxable Yield} =$$
$$\text{Tax Exempt Yield (Rate of Municipal)} \times \frac{1}{100\% - \text{Tax Rate}}$$

Table 5.2 shows the equivalent taxable yield on a municipal bond. For example, if you're in the 28th percentile tax bracket and invest in a six percent municipal bond, the equivalent taxable yield is 8.3 percent.

Companies such as Moody's Investors Service and Standard & Poor's rate municipal bonds on the "credit worthiness" of the issuer. Companies that are most credit worthy are rated "AAA" and the least credit worthy—companies that are in default—are rated "D."

Corporate bonds are more risky than other types of bonds, but they pay higher interest. Moody's and Standard & Poor's also rate corporate bonds.

The Mendoza's Social Security

Social Security is a comprehensive program of the federal government that covers retirement, survivor and disability benefits, as well as benefits for low-income elderly and disabled people. Some tend to believe that Social Security is a complete survivor, disability, and retirement program. However, it only provides a partial amount for these occurrences. Money for Social Security comes from both employee and employer contributions. Most employees are required to pay 6.2 percent of their wages up to a certain limit for Social Security and 1.45 percent of their wages with no limit for Medicare. Their employers are required to match the amount that they pay.

Your Social Security benefits depend on how much you earn during most of your working life. The more you earn, the larger your Social Security check will be. Both Durango and Brooke are taking early retirement at age 62. This means that they will receive a smaller Social Security check than if they wait until age 65. Durango will start collecting his Social Security in the amount of $1,118 per month later this year. Brooke will be 62 in two years, and she estimates her check will be around $900 a month.

Upon retirement, Durango and Brooke must make decisions within a short period of time about their health insurance coverage. Although they have **Medicare,** only part of the cost of their health care is covered. There are many types of private health coverage that pay for some or all of the health care costs not covered by Medicare. These types of insurance are called **supplemental coverage** and include **retiree coverage** (from a former employer or union) and **Medigap insurance** (from a private company or group). After studying the various types of supplemental coverage, Durango selects the retiree coverage from the company that he worked for during the last 30 years. Brooke is also covered as a dependent under this policy and can continue it if Durango dies before she does. He shared the cost of the insurance with his employer during his employment, but he must pay all of the cost of the insurance upon retirement.

The Mendoza's Pensions

In addition to personal investments and Social Security, many people count on pensions for retirement income. During a person's working years, contributions are made to an employer-sponsored fund. These funds are invested so

earnings will accumulate over the years. When employees retire, they begin receiving benefits.

Although the details of pension plans vary from company to company, there are two basic types—defined contribution plans and defined benefit plans. A **defined contribution plan** is a set amount added to the fund each month. The total benefit due to an employee depends on the contributions and earnings. In a **defined benefit plan** the employee is guaranteed a certain benefit, such as an amount equal to 50 percent of income from the final year worked. This defined benefit would continue each year for the rest of the person's life.

The funding of a particular pension plan depends on the company's policy. Some companies pay the entire contribution. At others, employees also make contributions. After a certain number of years, the benefits accumulated under a pension plan become the property of the employee. These funds are called **vested.** Once vested even employees who leave the company before normal retirement age receive their benefits.

Keywords

Treasury bonds – safest of all bonds; guaranteed by the U.S. government.

Series EE bonds – issued by the U.S. government, mature in 12 years, and have interest rates based on Treasury note yields.

Government agency bonds – created to help housing grow. Consist of high-quality mortgages.

Municipal bonds – exempt from federal income tax.

Corporate bonds – issued by corporations; usually more risky than other types of bonds.

Social Security – comprehensive program of the federal government, funded by employees and employers that provides for retirement, survivor, and disability coverage.

Medicare – health insurance coverage provided by the government for those 65 and older.

Supplemental coverage – private health insurance for retirees in addition to Medicare.

Retiree coverage – supplemental health insurance provided by a former employer or union.

Medigap insurance – supplemental health insurance provided by a private company or group.

Defined contribution plan – retirement plan whereby a set amount is added to the fund each month and the total benefit due depends on the contributions and earnings.

Defined benefit plan – retirement plan whereby the employee is guaranteed a certain benefit.

Vested – accumulated pension benefits that are the property of the employee.

Ridgeview Construction has a defined benefit pension plan that will pay Durango $1,200 a month when he retires. If Durango dies before Brooke, she will receive 75 percent of Durango's monthly check for as long as she lives.

Brooke has a Keogh retirement plan for herself and her employees at the card shop. You qualify for a **Keogh** if you're self-employed and earn money for work you do in addition to your regular job. If you have employees and you have a Keogh plan for yourself, you must provide benefits to your employees who qualify. Keoghs are set up as either defined contribution plans or defined benefit plans. You can customize the plan to suit your needs. Brooke's plan is set up as a defined contribution plan. She has $46,000 in it, which is included with stocks and mutual funds on the personal balance sheet. Like IRAs, withdrawals from Keoghs can be delayed until the covered person is 70½, and Brooke hopes to leave her Keogh money in a mutual fund until she reaches that age.

Keyword

Keogh – a retirement plan for the self-employed and small business owners.

Student Activities

Instructions: This section is designed for you to practice the concepts introduced in this unit. In the Student Activities, refer back to this unit if you need help calculating the equivalent yield on a municipal bond. You can also refer back to previous units for assistance on preparing a monthly budget, reading stock quotes, and recording transactions in a check register. Additionally, some of these activities may be completed either manually or automatically. The activities that merit automation include software directions.

You may use the Answer Sheet on pages 105 and 106 for activities not requiring FORMS. Remove the Answer Sheet before beginning the following activities and place it in your IN FILE. Once you have completed the activities place the Answer Sheet in the OUT FILE. Activities requiring FORMS include the page numbers of the FORMS and are filed appropriately in either the IN FILE or OUT FILE.

Activity 1

REQUIRED: Find the equivalent taxable yield on the following municipal bonds. Round to the nearest tenth of a percent.

Rate of Municipal	Tax Rate
7%	31%
4%	15%
8%	28%
10½%	28%
6½%	31%

Critical Thinking   If only one of the above bonds were rated AAA, which one do you think it would be and why?

_____

_____

_____

_____

_____

_____

_____

Activity 2

Maureen Cupick is a retired social worker for the state of Florida. She receives $1,325 a month from her pension and $785 in Social Security. She also has $50,000 in bonds that pay 12 percent. Interest on the bonds is automatically deposited into her checking account semi-annually. Her only other source of income is the interest from a $30,000 CD that she just renewed for another five years at a rate of eight percent simple interest. The interest from this CD is deposited into her checking account monthly. Maureen pays $800 a month for rent on her condo. All of her debts are paid. She spends $80 a month on gas and $70 a month on car insurance. Her food expense averages $400 a month and she pays approximately $200 a month for utilities. Maureen gives $150 a month to Holy Child Episcopal Church and $50 a month to Halifax Children's Home. She spends $100 a month on clothes and around $300 a month on travel and entertainment. Maureen's health care averages $250 a month. She budgets $200 for miscellaneous expenses. The rest of her income is budgeted for savings.

REQUIRED: Prepare a monthly budget on April 30 (FORM 26) for Maureen. (Note: Spread her bond income over 12 months.)

Software Directions

Refer back to Unit 1, Activity 2 for software directions on preparing a monthly budget.

Activity 3

The Port Henry Seniors investment club is considering investing in two stocks this month. They have $1,000 to invest. Table 5.3 is information pertaining to each of the stocks under consideration by the club.

REQUIRED: Answer the following questions about the stocks:
1. How many shares of each one of the stocks can the club buy at today's closing price? (Disregard any fees connected with the transaction.)
2. Which stock had the greater net change?
3. Which stock traded more shares today?
4. Which stock paid the higher dividend per share?
5. Which stock would you recommend the club buy?

Activity 4

Judy and Louis Moore retired last year. They were both 65 and eligible for Social Security and Medicare. Their combined retirement income including Social Security, pensions, and investment income is $5,300 a month. After thoroughly studying their alternatives, they finally narrowed their choice to the following two supplementary policies:

Policy A: This policy is provided by Judy's employer and can cover the Moores. The premium is $400 a month with no limit on annual increases. If either Judy or Louis dies, the premium does not change. This policy will cover everything that Medicare does including preexisting conditions. Judy has a damaged heart valve that could require surgery in the future. This is considered a preexisting condition.

Policy B: This policy is provided by Louis's union and can cover both Judy and Louis. The premium is $400 a month with no limit on annual increases. If either Judy or Louis dies, the premium does not change. This policy covers everything that Medicare does. However, preexisting conditions are covered after three years.

REQUIRED: Which of the two policies should Judy and Louis select?

Table 5.3											
52-week					**Yld**		**Vol**				**Net**
Hi	**Lo**	**Stock**	**Sym**	**Div**	**%**	**PE**	**100s**	**Hi**	**Lo**	**Close**	**Chg**
50¹⁵⁄₁₆	30⅛	Emru	EM	.25	1.5	18	120	48½	48	48¼	+¼
18½	15¼	Davis Ray	DRA	.10	1.8	12	22	18	17½	17¾	-½

What are some major factors Judy and Louis should consider when making their choice of health insurance policies?

_____

_____

_____

_____

_____

_____

_____

_____

COMPREHENSIVE PROBLEM

The Mendozas have gathered the following information in connection with their finances after Durango retires. Brooke's investment club money ($11,000) and her Keogh ($46,000) will remain untouched and hopefully continue to grow. The remaining money they had in the stock market ($178,000) was transferred to municipal bonds that pay an annual rate of six percent.

Durango has started collecting his $1,118 monthly Social Security check and his $1,200 monthly pension from Ridgeview Construction Company. Brooke's take-home pay after taxes from the card shop is $1,500 each month. Their monthly expenses include the following: real estate taxes, $200; homeowner's insurance, $50; medical insurance, $450; other medical expenses, $100; electric, $150; telephone, $50; water, $30; cable, $50; food, $600; gas, $150; car insurance, $100; investment club, $100; contributions, $200; gifts, $100; travel and entertainment, $1,500; and miscellaneous expense, $300.

They are not sure what the remainder will be spent on or if all of the estimates are accurate. Show this amount temporarily as a balance available for savings on the monthly budget. The Mendozas opened a new senior citizen checking account at Ridgeview State Bank. This account has no monthly service charge.

PART 1

REQUIRED: Prepare a monthly budget (FORM 27) on October 31 for the Mendozas.

Software Directions

Refer back to Unit 1, Activity 2 for software directions on preparing a monthly budget.

If the Mendozas have money left over at the end of the month, what should they do with it?

_____

_____

_____

_____

_____

_____

_____

_____

PART 2

REQUIRED: Record the following transactions in the Mendoza's check register. Remove the check register from page 127. (Reminder: Do not write checks or make out deposit slips.)

CHECKING ACCOUNT TRANSACTIONS

11-4   Deposited Durango's pension check ($1,200) and Social Security check ($1,118) to open the new account.

11-5   Brooke withdrew $300 from an ATM.

11-8   Transferred $250 from their checking account to a savings account in Ridgeview Savings Bank to go toward real estate taxes ($200) and home insurance ($50). (Reminder: The transaction is entered as a set-aside for the two items.)

11-9   Durango withdrew $200 from an ATM.

11-14   Check No. 101 to RCC (FORM 28) for medical insurance.

11-15   Deposited Brooke's $1,500 paycheck from the card shop. Brooke had a crown put on her tooth. Check No. 102 to Greg McFee, DDS. (FORM 29)

11-19   Check No. 103 to Ridgeview Electric Company monthly electric bill for $108.50.

11-20 Brooke withdrew $200 from an ATM.

11-21 Durango had an eye exam that is not covered under his medical insurance. Check No.104 to Sterling Optical for $85.

11-22 Check No.105 to Mid-West Telephone Company for monthly telephone bill for $87.20.

11-23 Check No.106 to Ridgeview Water System (FORM 30) for monthly water bill.

11-24 Check No.107 to Washburn Cable, Inc., for monthly TV cable bill for $50.

11-25 Durango withdrew $300 from an ATM.

11-26 Check No.108 to Geico for the Mendoza's monthly car insurance premium for $100.

11-26 Deposited $890.00 from municipal bond interest.

11-27 Check No.109 to Holiday Cruise Lines (FORM 31) for the Mendoza's vacation cruise.

11-28 Check No.110 to Ridgeview Investment Club for $100.

11-29 Check No.111 to March of Dimes for $100.

11-30 Check No.112 to Wildlife Preservation Fund for $100.

11-30 Check No.113 to Toys-R-Us for $239.70.

PART 3

REQUIRED: Prepare a financial record sheet (FORM 32) based on the entries in the check register prepared in Part 2. Before bringing down the column totals, the following summary of the cash record sheet is entered on the last line in the financial record sheet: food $560, travel & entertainment $106, gas for car $133, clothing $128, and miscellaneous $55. ATM withdrawals for $1,000 recorded in the check register during November were used for these items. Special Note: follow these steps.

Step 1. Add the Withdrawal and Payments column totals.

Step 2. Add totals of all eight columns beginning with Clothing and ending with Savings/Investments.

Step 3. Subtract the total computed in Step 2 from the total computed in Step 1. You should have a balance of $18. Show this amount at the bottom of the financial record sheet as Ending Cash Balance, $18.

Software Directions

Here is how to prepare a financial record sheet in a spreadsheet program:

1. Begin a new workbook.
2. Begin by entering each column title in the top row.
3. Select an entire column by clicking the column letter noted in gray and move the mouse over the column edge. Pressing and holding the left mouse button, adjust the column width to your desired specifications, or double-click the button on the edge of the column to automatically fit each column.
4. For each row, enter the daily activity into the designated column for each particular column classification.
5. After entering the daily activity into the workbook, sum the totals of each column by selecting the cell under the final entry of each column. Click on the summation symbol at the top of the toolbar. Select all activity in the corresponding column for summation.
6. Finally, double underline all totals in the workbook to designate that each cell is a summation of the activity above. Utilize the underline tool on the formatting toolbar at the top of your screen. To activate the formatting tool bar, hover the mouse pointer over the top of the screen and right click. Select **formatting**. Choose the type of underline as needed.

PART 4

REQUIRED: Prepare a budget comparison sheet (FORM 33) for the Mendozas using amounts from the monthly budget prepared in Part 1 and amounts in the financial record sheet prepared in Part 3.

Software Directions

Refer back to Step 6 in the Comprehensive Problem in Unit 1 to see how to prepare a budget comparison sheet using software.

Forms

PERSONAL BALANCE SHEET

Student's Name _____ Date _____

_____

_____

_____

_____

ASSETS

Checking Account   _____

Savings Account   _____

Furniture   _____

Computer   _____

Stereo   _____

Vehicle   _____

Total Assets   _____

LIABILITIES

Computer & Stereo Loan   _____

Student Loan   _____

Total Liabilities   _____

NET WORTH   _____

Total Liabilities and Net Worth   _____

MONTHLY BUDGET

Student's Name _____ Date _____

_____

_____
_____
_____

INCOME

    Take Home Pay _____

EXPENSES

    Rent _____

    Utilities _____

    Food _____

    Travel & Entertainment _____

    Clothing _____

    Gas _____

    Car Insurance _____

    Contributions _____

    Life Insurance _____

    Computer & Stereo Loan _____

    Student Loan _____

    Miscellaneous _____

      Total Expenses _____

Balance Available for Savings _____

SOUTHERN BELL TELEPHONE COMPANY

Len Lombardo
1795 Ocean View Drive
Daytona Beach, FL 32016

Account No. 0443-5765-02

Amount Due by 4/30/20-- **$65.40**

Send payment (no cash) to:
SOUTHERN BELL TELEPHONE COMPANY
144 SOUTHERN BELL TERRANCE
DAYTONA, FL. 32018

Note: Write your telephone number on your check.

------- Keep this part for your records -------

Past Month:

Past Amount $55.80
Amount Received $55.80
Past Due Amount . . . . $ -0-

Current Month:

Monthly Local Service $22.60
Other Services including Taxes (See Enclosed) $11.50
Monthly Long Distance Service $31.30
Total Balance $65.40

TO: **Len Lombardo**
1795 Ocean View Drive
Daytona Beach, FL 32016

MAKE YOUR CHECK PAYABLE TO:
GEICO
1249 Main Avenue South
Miami, FL 73120

8XDFQ1289
PAY: $375.00

- -

Keep this portion for your records

Policy No. **8XDFQ1389**

Last Day to Pay: **4/15/20--**

Amount Due: **$375.00**

Summary:
Preferred Customer
Insures More Than One Auto
Positive Safety Record

GEICO
Auto Insurance
"At It's Best"

(See Enclosed Sheets for Detailed Policy Information)

FOR CLASSROOM USE ONLY
REFUND CHECK

Check No. _2001_

Date _April 1, 20--_

TO THE
ORDER OF _Len Lombardo_

$ _$ 802.00_

Eight hundred two and 00/100 DOLLARS

NON-NEGOTIABLE

U.S. TREASURY

Bank of Commerce
Atlanta, GA 30361

Memo _____

Mary Taylor

⑆085920076⑆ 30 ⑆4100056⑆ 01   612-12/47

FLORIDA POWER & LIGHT

PO Box 8199
Jacksonville, FL 32205

STATEMENT

Account No. **22314267895**
April 1, 20--

Len Lombardo
1795 Ocean View Drive
Daytona Beach, FL 32016

METER READING: 1980 KWH
Amount Due: **$131.52**

2291324499 4334 34020 0000000

~ Halifax Cable Company ~
360 Beach Road
Daytona Beach, FL 32016

Customer: Len Lombardo, 1795 Ocean View Drive, Daytona Beach, FL 32016
Customer No. 994

Description: Basic Home Cable Service

One Week FREE movie channels with
an opportunity for special discount offers.
(Telephone 904-225-8001)

Amount Due: **$37.50**

We Appreciate Serving You.

BANK RECONCILIATION FORM

Student's Name _____ Date _____

_____

_____

_____

_____

Bank Statement
Balance _____

ADD:
Deposits in Transit _____
Total _____

SUBTRACT:
Outstanding Checks _____
  and Other Deductions _____

_____

_____ _____

Adjusted Bank Balance _____

Checkbook Balance _____
Add Interest _____
Total _____
Deduct Bank Fees _____
Adjusted Checkbook Balance _____

PERSONAL BALANCE SHEET

Student's Name _____ Date _____

_____

_____

_____

_____

ASSETS

    Checking Account   _____

    Savings Account   _____

    Vehicle   _____

    Computer   _____

    Furniture   _____

    Other Assets   _____

       Total Assets   _____

LIABILITIES

    Student Loan   _____

       Total Liabilities   _____

NET WORTH   _____

    Total Liabilities and Net Worth   _____

MONTHLY BUDGET

Student's Name _____ Date _____

_____

_____

_____

_____

INCOME

    Take Home Pay   _____

    From Savings   _____

    From Jerome   _____

      Total Income   _____

EXPENSES

    Rent   _____

    Food   _____

    Entertainment   _____

    Clothing   _____

    Electric   _____

    Gas   _____

    Telephone   _____

    Miscellaneous   _____

      Total Expenses   _____

BANK RECONCILIATION FORM

Student's Name _____ Date _____

_____

_____

_____

_____

_____

Bank Statement
Balance   _____

ADD:
Deposits in Transit   _____
Total   _____

SUBTRACT:
Outstanding Checks   _____
  and Other Deductions   _____

                            _____
                            _____   _____

Adjusted Bank Balance   _____

Checkbook Balance   _____
Add Interest   _____
Total   _____
Deduct Bank Fees   _____
Adjusted Checkbook Balance   _____

CASH RECORD SHEET

Student's Name _____

Date _____

Date	Description	Cash Withdrawals	Payments	Clothing	Entertainment	Food	Housing	Transportation	Miscellaneous

FINANCIAL RECORD SHEET

Student's Name _____

Date	Chk.	Description	Receipts	Withdrawals	Payments	Clothing	Entertainment	Food	Health Care	Housing	Transportation	Miscellaneous	Savings/Investments

Date _____

BUDGET COMPARISON SHEET

Student's Name _____ Date _____

_____
_____

_____
_____
_____

CATEGORY	ESTIMATED	ACTUAL	VARIANCE
INCOME:	_____	_____	_____
EXPENSES:			
Rent	_____	_____	_____
Food	_____	_____	_____
Entertainment	_____	_____	_____
Clothing	_____	_____	_____
Electric	_____	_____	_____
Gas	_____	_____	_____
Telephone	_____	_____	_____
Miscellaneous	_____	_____	_____
Totals	_____	_____	_____

Student's Name _____　Date _____

Activity 1

Step 1:_____

_____

_____

_____

_____ (Days in billing period)

Step 2:_____

_____

_____

_____

_____ (Total of each day's balances)

Step 3: $ _____(average daily balance)

Step 4: $ _____(monthly finance charge)

Activity 2

$ _____amount of the down payment

$ _____amount financed

$ _____amount of the installment payments

$ _____total cost of the boat

$ _____finance charge

Activity 3

1. Tyrone's out-of-pocket expenses:

_____deductible

_____(5-23)

_____(5-24)

_____(6-15)

_____(6-15)

_____(10-20)

_____(10-22)

_____(12-1)

_____(12-4)

_____(12 Premiums)

_____(Total)

2. Emily's out-of-pocket expenses:

_____deductible

_____(11-14)

_____(11-14)

_____(12-15)

_____(12-16)

_____(12-16)

_____(12 Premiums)

_____(Total)

3. $_____Total out-of-pocket expenses for Tyrone and Emily

4. $_____Monthly budget medical expenses for Tyrone and Emily

Activity 4:

$ _____Option 1

$ _____Option 2

$ _____Option 3

Choice you would select for one-year deposit_____

_____

Comprehensive Problem:

1. $_____Sears finance charge

   $_____Dillards finance charge

   $_____Visa finance charge

2. $_____amount that can be withdrawn from savings (excess of $2,500)

   $_____balance left on Sears credit card

   $_____balance left on Dillards credit card

   $_____balance left on Visa credit card

3. Where Miller's should deposit their checking account? _____

   _____

   _____

   Where Miller's should deposit their savings account? _____

   _____

   _____

PERSONAL BALANCE SHEET

Student's Name _____ Date _____

_____
_____

_____
_____
_____

ASSETS

    Checking Account   _____

    Savings–The Millers   _____

    Car   _____

    Truck   _____

    Furniture   _____

        Total Assets   _____

LIABILITIES

    Truck Loan   _____

    Dillards Credit Card   _____

    Visa Credit Card   _____

        Total Liabilities   _____

NET WORTH   _____

    Total Liabilities and Net Worth   _____

MONTHLY BUDGET

Student's Name _____ Date _____

_____

_____

_____

INCOME

Take Home Pay _____

EXPENSES

Rent _____

Food _____

Vacation & Entertainment _____

Clothing _____

Car Insurance _____

Utilities _____

Credit Card Payments _____

Gas _____

Truck Loan _____

Medical Expenses _____

Cable TV _____

Disability Insurance _____

Charitable Contributions _____

Educational Expenses _____

Miscellaneous _____

Total Expenses _____

Balance Available for Savings _____

Student's Name _____ Date _____

Activity 1

$ _____amount of the loan

$ _____amount of Yuma's monthly payment

$ _____amount of Yuma's interest over the life of the loan

Activity 2

$ _____amount of the Kaufmans' loan

$ _____amount of monthly payments with Major Bank & Trust

$ _____amount of monthly payments with First National Bank

$ _____total amount of interest paid with Major Bank & Trust

$ _____total amount of interest paid with First National Bank

Activity 3

$ _____ property tax on Division Road

$ _____ property tax on West & Center

$ _____ property tax on Fifth Street

$ _____ property tax on Nebraska Avenue

$ _____ property tax on Milton Drive

Activity 4

$_____ Bell's monthly payment (include principal, interest, taxes, and insurance)

Comprehensive Problem

This activity requires the use of FORMS only.

FINANCIAL RECORD SHEET

The Expanding Family

Student's Name _____

Date _____

Date	Chk.	Description	Receipts	Withdrawals	Payments	Clothing	Entertainment	Food	Health Care	Housing	Transportation	Miscellaneous	Savings/ Investments

MONTHLY BUDGET

Student's Name _____ Date _____

_____

_____
_____
_____

INCOME

    Take Home Pay _____

EXPENSES

    Home Mortgage _____

    Food _____

    Entertainment _____

    Clothing _____

    Car Payment _____

    Utilities _____

    Set-asides _____

    Gas _____

    Other Car Expense _____

    Health Care _____

    Charitable Contributions _____

    Sister's College Expenses _____

    Miscellaneous _____

        Total Expenses _____

        Balance Available for Savings _____

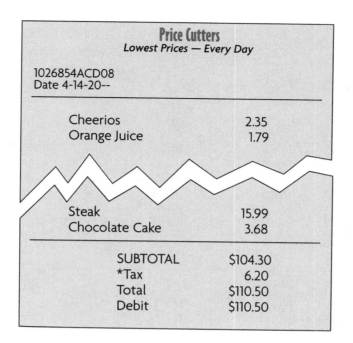

Price Cutters
Lowest Prices — Every Day

1026854ACD08
Date 4-14-20--

Cheerios	2.35
Orange Juice	1.79
Steak	15.99
Chocolate Cake	3.68

SUBTOTAL	$104.30
*Tax	6.20
Total	$110.50
Debit	$110.50

Marathon Credit Union

Payment 25

DATE:	4/1/20--
ACCOUNT NO.:	689-0457
AMOUNT DUE:	$ 337.00
ACCOUNT BALANCE:	$8088.00

Lou Allendes
15574 Canyo Road
McAllen, Texas

Amount Due 4/15/20--
Account No. 444-56-873

EASTERN BELL
Green Acres Plaza
Fayetteville, AR 72701

EASTERN BELL

This portion is for your records

Monthly Service	$39.20
Monthly Maintenance	$ 3.00
Federal Tax	$ .89
State and Local Taxes	$ 2.24
Balance Due	**$45.33**

EASTERN BELL

Premium Power Company

P.O. Box 1405
McAllen, Texas 72702

LOU ALLENDES
15574 Randon Road
McAllen, Texas 72702

Please detach and mail
this portion with your
payment.

Total Amount Due: $124.50
Due Date: April 25, 20--

- -

This bill is delinquent if payment is not received by the due date—retain lower portion for your records

Name:	Lou Allendes
Account Number:	21019-001
Location number:	28-04-8800
Phone number:	(501) 448-7624
Billing date:	APR 1, 20--
Rate:	APR 25, 20--

Meter Readings

Present	Previous	KWH Usage	Billing Period	Days
2353	–0–	2352	3/01/20-- to 3/31/20--	29

AVERAGE DAILY KWH USAGE 81.13

Student's Name _____   Date _____

Activity 1

$ _____1. Highest price for Brown & Brown sold during the last 52 weeks.

$ _____2. Number of shares Brown & Brown traded on this day.

$ _____3. Brown & Brown's P-E ratio.

$ _____4. Amount of money Fortner made on Brown & Brown stock between yesterday and today.

$ _____5. Last price that Brunswick traded for the day.

$ _____6. Amount Fortner paid for 200 shares of Brunswick at its lowest price during the past 52 weeks.

$ _____7. Amount of total dividends on 1,000 shares of Brunswick last year.

$ _____8. Amount for 100 shares of Brunswick just as the market closed.

Activity 2

_____ EFU's P-E ratio

_____ FMK's P-E ratio

_____ HDL's P-E ratio

_____ THX's P-E ratio

_____ PXP's P-E ratio

Activity 3

_____1. Current yield higher or lower than the interest rate on the Chase bonds.

_____2. Number of IBM bonds sold on this day.

_____3. Date the Chase bonds mature.

_____4. IBM bonds closed higher or lower than yesterday.

_____5. Amount in dollars for annual interest paid on each one of Antonio's Chase bonds.

Activity 4

This activity requires the use of FORMS.

Comprehensive Problem:

$ _____1. Amount of money left in Lucy's savings account after the condo transactions.

$ _____2. Monthly mortgage (principal and interest) payments for Lucy.

$ _____3. Amount in Jessica's money market trust fund at the end of five years.

Parts 4 and 5 require the use of FORMS only.

Form
1040A

Department of the Treasury–Internal Revenue Service

U.S. Individual Income Tax Return (99) **2000**   IRS Use Only–Do not write or staple in this space.

Label
(See page 20.)

OMB No. 1545-0085

**Use the
IRS label.**

Otherwise,
please print
or type.

L A B E L   H E R E

Your first name and initial	Last name

Your social security number

If a joint return, spouse's first name and initial	Last name

Spouse's social security number

Home address (number and street). If you have a P.O. box, see page 21.   Apt. no.

City, town or post office, state, and ZIP code. If you have a foreign address, see page 21.

▲ **Important!** ▲
You **must** enter your
SSN(s) above.

**Presidential
Election Campaign**
(See page 21.) ▶

Note. Checking "Yes" will not change your tax or reduce your refund.
Do you, or your spouse if filing a joint return, want $3 to go to this fund? . . . . ▶

You   Spouse
☐ Yes ☐ No   ☐ Yes ☐ No

**Filing
status**

Check only
one box.

1 ☐ Single
2 ☐ Married filing joint return (even if only one had income)
3 ☐ Married filing separate return. Enter spouse's social security number above and full name here. ▶ _____
4 ☐ Head of household (with qualifying person). (See page 22.) If the qualifying person is a child but not your dependent, enter this child's name here. ▶ _____
5 ☐ Qualifying widow(er) with dependent child (year spouse died ▶ _____). (See page 23.)

Exemptions

If more than
seven
dependents,
see page 23.

6a ☐ **Yourself.** If your parent (or someone else) can claim you as a dependent on his or her tax return, **do not** check box 6a.

b ☐ **Spouse**

**No. of boxes
checked on
6a and 6b** _____

c **Dependents:**

(1) First name Last name	(2) Dependent's social security number	(3) Dependent's relationship to you	(4) ✔ if qualifying child for child tax credit (see page 24)
	⋮		☐
	⋮		☐
	⋮		☐
	⋮		☐
	⋮		☐
	⋮		☐

**No. of your
children on
6c who:**
• **lived with
you** _____
• **did not live
with you due
to divorce or
separation**
(see page 25) _____

**Dependents
on 6c not
entered above** _____

d Total number of exemptions claimed.

**Add numbers
entered on
lines above** ☐

Income

**Attach
Form(s) W-2
here. Also
attach
Form(s)
1099-R if tax
was withheld.**

If you did not
get a W-2, see
page 26.

Enclose, but do
not attach, any
payment.

7 Wages, salaries, tips, etc. Attach Form(s) W-2.   7

8a **Taxable** interest. Attach Schedule 1 if required.   8a
  b **Tax-exempt** interest. **Do not** include on line 8a.   8b
9 Ordinary dividends. Attach Schedule 1 if required.   9

10 Capital gain distributions (see page 26).   10

11a Total IRA distributions.   11a   **11b** Taxable amount (see page 26).   11b

12a Total pensions and annuities.   12a   **12b** Taxable amount (see page 27).   12b

13 Unemployment compensation, qualified state tuition program earnings, and Alaska Permanent Fund dividends.   13

14a Social security benefits.   14a   **14b** Taxable amount (see page 29).   14b

15 Add lines 7 through 14b (far right column). This is your **total income.** ▶ 15

**Adjusted
gross
income**

16 IRA deduction (see page 31).   16
17 Student loan interest deduction (see page 31).   17
18 Add lines 16 and 17. These are your **total adjustments.**   18

19 Subtract line 18 from line 15. This is your **adjusted gross income.** ▶ 19

For Disclosure, Privacy Act, and Paperwork Reduction Act Notice, see page 55.   Cat. No. 11327A   Form **1040A** (2000)

Form 1040A (2000)

Taxable income	**20**	Enter the amount from line 19.		20
	21a	Check if: ☐ **You** were 65 or older　☐ Blind　**Enter number of** ☐ **Spouse** was 65 or older　☐ Blind　**boxes checked ▶** 21a ☐		
	b	If you are married filing separately and your spouse itemizes deductions, see page 33 and check here . . . . ▶ 21b ☐		
	22	Enter the **standard deduction** for your filing status. **But** see page 33 if you checked any box on line 21a or 21b **or** if someone can claim you as a dependent. • Single—$4,400　• Married filing jointly or Qualifying widow(er)—$7,350 • Head of household—$6,450　• Married filing separately—$3,675		22
	23	Subtract line 22 from line 20. If line 22 is more than line 20, enter -0-.		23
	24	Multiply $2,800 by the total number of exemptions claimed on line 6d.		24
	25	Subtract line 24 from line 23. If line 24 is more than line 23, enter -0-. This is your **taxable income**.　　　　　　　　　　▶		25
Tax, credits, and payments	**26**	**Tax** (see page 34).		26
	27	Credit for child and dependent care expenses. Attach Schedule 2.	27	
	28	Credit for the elderly or the disabled. Attach Schedule 3.	28	
	29	Education credits. Attach Form 8863.	29	
	30	Child tax credit (see page 37).	30	
	31	Adoption credit. Attach Form 8839.	31	
	32	Add lines 27 through 31. These are your **total credits**.		32
	33	Subtract line 32 from line 26. If line 32 is more than line 26, enter -0-.		33
	34	Advance earned income credit payments from Form(s) W-2.		34
	35	Add lines 33 and 34. This is your **total tax**.　　　　▶		35
	36	Federal income tax withheld from Forms W-2 and 1099.	36	
	37	2000 estimated tax payments and amount applied from 1999 return.	37	
If you have a qualifying child, attach Schedule EIC.	**38a**	**Earned income credit (EIC).**	38a	
	b	Nontaxable earned income: amount ▶ ┃ and type ▶		
	39	Additional child tax credit. Attach Form 8812.	39	
	40	Add lines 36, 37, 38a, and 39. These are your **total payments**.　▶		40
Refund	**41**	If line 40 is more than line 35, subtract line 35 from line 40. This is the amount you **overpaid**.		41
Have it directly deposited! See page 48 and fill in 42b, 42c, and 42d.	**42a**	Amount of line 41 you want **refunded to you**.		42a
	▶ **b**	Routing number ┃┃┃┃┃┃┃┃┃　▶ **c** Type: ☐ Checking　☐ Savings		
	▶ **d**	Account number ┃┃┃┃┃┃┃┃┃┃┃┃┃┃┃┃┃		
	43	Amount of line 41 you want **applied to your 2001 estimated tax.**	43	
Amount you owe	**44**	If line 35 is more than line 40, subtract line 40 from line 35. This is the **amount you owe.** For details on how to pay, see page 49.		44
	45	Estimated tax penalty (see page 49).	45	

Sign here Joint return? See page 21. Keep a copy for your records.	Under penalties of perjury, I declare that I have examined this return and accompanying schedules and statements, and to the best of my knowledge and belief, they are true, correct, and accurately list all amounts and sources of income I received during the tax year. Declaration of preparer (other than the taxpayer) is based on all information of which the preparer has any knowledge.

Your signature	Date	Your occupation	Daytime phone number ( )
Spouse's signature. If a joint return, **both** must sign.	Date	Spouse's occupation	May the IRS discuss this return with the preparer shown below (see page 50)? ☐ **Yes** ☐ **No**

Paid preparer's use only	Preparer's signature ▶	Date	Check if self-employed ☐ / Preparer's SSN or PTIN
	Firm's name (or yours if self-employed), address, and ZIP code ▶		EIN ┊ / Phone no. ( )

Form **1040A** (2000)

PERSONAL BALANCE SHEET

Student's Name _____ Date _____

_____
_____

_____
_____
_____

ASSETS

    Checking Account   _____

    Savings Account   _____

    Condo   _____

    Furniture   _____

    Car   _____

    Other Assets   _____

      Total Assets   _____

LIABILITIES

    Mortgage   _____

      Total Liabilities   _____

NET WORTH

  Total Liabilities and Net Worth   _____

MONTHLY BUDGET

Student's Name _____ Date _____

_____

_____

_____

_____

INCOME

Take Home Pay   _____

Interest from Savings   _____

Total Income   _____

EXPENSES

Mortgage   _____

Real Estate Tax   _____

Residential Insurance   _____

Food   _____

Travel & Entertainment   _____

Clothing   _____

Car Insurance   _____

Electric   _____

Gas   _____

Telephone   _____

Tuition   _____

Miscellaneous   _____

Total Expenses   _____

Balance Available for Savings   _____

Student's Name _____   Date _____

Activity 1

_____   equivalent taxable yield (municipal rate 7%/tax rate 31%)

_____   equivalent taxable yield (municipal rate 4%/tax rate 15%)

_____   equivalent taxable yield (municipal rate 8%/tax rate 28%)

_____   equivalent taxable yield (municipal rate 10½%/tax rate 28%)

_____   equivalent taxable yield (municipal rate 6½%/tax rate 31%)

Activity 2

This activity requires the use of FORMS only.

Activity 3

_____ 1. Number of shares of Emru the club can buy at today's closing.

_____   Number of shares of Davis Ray the club can buy at today's closing.

_____ 2. Stock with the greater net change.

_____ 3. Stock which traded more shares today.

_____ 4. Stock which paid the higher dividend per share.

_____ 5. Stock which you would recommend the club buy.

Activity 4

_____The policy Judy and Louis should select.

Comprehensive Problem

This problem requires the use of FORMS only.

MONTHLY BUDGET

Student's Name _____ Date _____

_____

_____

_____

_____

INCOME

Pension   _____

Social Security   _____

Bond Interest   _____

CD Interest   _____

Total Income   _____

EXPENSES

Rent   _____

Gas   _____

Food   _____

Car Insurance   _____

Food   _____

Utilities   _____

Contributions   _____

Clothes   _____

Travel & Entertainment   _____

Health Care   _____

Miscellaneous Expense   _____

Total Expenses   _____

Balance Available for Savings   _____

MONTHLY BUDGET

Student's Name _____ Date _____

_____

_____

_____

INCOME

    Municipal Bond Interest   _____

    Social Security   _____

    Pension   _____

    Take Home Pay   _____

        Total Income   _____

EXPENSES

    Real Estate Taxes   _____

    Homeowner's Insurance   _____

    Medical Insurance   _____

    Other Medical Expenses   _____

    Electric   _____

    Telephone   _____

    Water   _____

    Cable   _____

    Food   _____

    Gas   _____

    Car Insurance   _____

    Investment Club   _____

    Contributions   _____

    Gifts   _____

    Travel & Entertainment   _____

    Miscellaneous Expense   _____

        Total Expenses   _____

Balance Available for Savings   _____

Account Information
Account Number: MPV-114
Date Due: 12/01/20--
Amount Due: $450.00

Customer Information
Durango and Brooke Mendoza
2222 Newton Avenue
Ridgeview, IN 46625

Send Payment To:

Ridgeview Construction Company
7643 Madison Avenue
South Bend, IN 46606

Make Check Payable To: **RCC Insurance**

Send this portion with payment.

Keep this portion with your records.

RCC Insurance

Description: Medical Insurance
Amount: $450.00
Total: $450.00

Account Number: MPV-114
Date Due: 12/01/20--

Durango and Brooke Mendoza
2222 Newton Avenue
Ridgeview, IN 46625

Dr. Greg McFee, DDS
#13 Mesa Avenue
Ridgeview, IN 46625

STATEMENT OF SERVICES & CHARGES

Client #:	5578
Date:	11/15
Provider:	McFee
Provider Phone:	219-587-8877
License #:	2298
Tax ID #:	71-1728099

To: **Brooke Mendoza**
2222 Newton Avenue
Ridgeview, IN 46625

Patient: Brooke Mendoza

Service Date	Description	Fee	Balance
11/15	Crown	300.00	300.00
	Patient Total Charges		300.00

Detach Here

Amount Due: $300.00	Patient #: 5578	Statement Date: 11/15
Amount Enclosed: _____	Check #: _____	Patient: Brooke Mendoza

Brooke Mendoza
2222 Newton Avenue
Ridgeview, IN 46625

Dr. Greg McFee, DDS
#13 Mesa Avenue
Ridgeview, IN 46625

RIDGEVIEW WATER SYSTEM
1365 West Olive   Ridgeview, IN 46625

SERVICE ADDRESS: 2222 Newton Avenue

DATES SERVICED		DATE BILLED		ACCOUNT NO.	DATE DUE:
10/15 to 11/15		11/18		548-7882	12/5

Pres. Read	Prev. Read	Usage-100 Gals.	Code	Amount	
9255	9105	150	W	31.67	
		150	S	27.37	
Taxes				2.96	

Amount Due   **$62.00**

Please Return This Stub With Payment

Account No.:   548-7882-32
Amount Due: $62.00
Due Date: 12/5

Durango and Brooke Mendoza
2222 Newton Avenue
Ridgeview, IN 46625

Holiday Cruise Lines

986 Cardinal Court
South Bend,. IN 46602

INVOICE

Passengers Information:
Durango and Brooke Mendoza
2222 Newton Avenue
Ridgeview, IN 46625
219-623-5574

We hope you enjoy your cruise!

If you have any questions, please call us

at 1-800-958-2469

Dates of Travel: 03/15/20-- – 03/18/20--
Cruise Title: Bahama SeaBreaze

Amount Due: $1,150

Retain this invoice for your records

Bahama SeaBreaze Cruise
03/15/20-- – 03/18/20--
$1,150 due on 112/10

Holiday Cruise Lines
986 Cardinal Court
South Bend, IN 46602

Durango & Brooke Mendoza
2222 Newton Avenue
Ridgeview, IN 46625

Amount Enclosed $_____

FINANCIAL RECORD SHEET

The Older Married Couple

Student's Name _____

Date _____

Date	Chk.	Description	Receipts	Withdrawals	Payments	Clothing	Entertainment	Food	Health Care	Housing	Transportation	Miscellaneous	Savings/ Investments

BUDGET COMPARISON SHEET

Student's Name _____ Date _____

_____

_____
_____
_____

CATEGORY	ESTIMATED	ACTUAL	VARIANCE
INCOME:	$_____	$_____	$_____
EXPENSES:			
Real Estate Taxes	$_____	$_____	$_____
Home Insurance	_____	_____	_____
Medical Insurance	_____	_____	_____
Other Medical Exp.	_____	_____	_____
Electric	_____	_____	_____
Telephone	_____	_____	_____
Water	_____	_____	_____
Cable	_____	_____	_____
Food	_____	_____	_____
Gas	_____	_____	_____
Car Insurance	_____	_____	_____
Investment Club	_____	_____	_____
Contributions	_____	_____	_____
Gifts	_____	_____	_____
Travel & Enter.	_____	_____	_____
Clothing	_____	_____	_____
Miscellaneous Exp.	_____	_____	_____
Totals	$_____	$_____	$_____
SAVINGS	$_____	$_____	$_____

Blank Forms

Check No.	Date	Checks Issued To or Description of Deposit	Payments	✓	Deposit	Balance
	4/1/15	Check			256 30	

Check No.	Date	Checks Issued To or Description of Deposit	Payments	✓	Deposit	Balance

Check No. 101

No. 101

5-94
812

_____
_____

_____ 20--

PAY TO THE
ORDER OF _____ $ _____

_____ DOLLARS

FOR USE IN CLASSROOM ONLY

FIRST NATIONAL BANK OF DAYTONA BEACH
DAYTONA BEACH, FL 32016

MEMO _____

⑈07820076⒉ 20:4800056 ⑊101

Check No. 102

No. 102

5-94
812

_____
_____

_____ 20--

PAY TO THE
ORDER OF _____ $ _____

_____ DOLLARS

FOR USE IN CLASSROOM ONLY

FIRST NATIONAL BANK OF DAYTONA BEACH
DAYTONA BEACH, FL 32016

MEMO _____

⑈07820076⒉ 20:4800056 ⑊102

Check No. 103

No. 103

5-94
812

_____
_____

_____ 20--

PAY TO THE
ORDER OF _____ $ _____

_____ DOLLARS

FOR USE IN CLASSROOM ONLY

FIRST NATIONAL BANK OF DAYTONA BEACH
DAYTONA BEACH, FL 32016

MEMO _____

⑈07820076⒉ 20:4800056 ⑊103

Check No. 104

No. 104

5-94
812

20--

PAY TO THE
ORDER OF _____ $ _____

_____ DOLLARS

FOR USE IN CLASSROOM ONLY

FIRST NATIONAL BANK OF DAYTONA BEACH
DAYTONA BEACH, FL 32016

MEMO _____

⑆07820076⑆ 20⑈4800056 ⑆104

Check No. 105

No. 105

5-94
812

20--

PAY TO THE
ORDER OF _____ $ _____

_____ DOLLARS

FOR USE IN CLASSROOM ONLY

FIRST NATIONAL BANK OF DAYTONA BEACH
DAYTONA BEACH, FL 32016

MEMO _____

⑆07820076⑆ 20⑈4800056 ⑆105

Check No. 106

No. 106

5-94
812

20--

PAY TO THE
ORDER OF _____ $ _____

_____ DOLLARS

FOR USE IN CLASSROOM ONLY

FIRST NATIONAL BANK OF DAYTONA BEACH
DAYTONA BEACH, FL 32016

MEMO _____

⑆07820076⑆ 20⑈4800056 ⑆106

No. 107

5-94
812

20--

PAY TO THE
ORDER OF _____ $ _____

_____ DOLLARS

FOR USE IN CLASSROOM ONLY

FIRST NATIONAL BANK OF DAYTONA BEACH
DAYTONA BEACH, FL 32016

MEMO _____

⑆07820076⑆ 20⑈480056⑈ ⑉107

No. 108

5-94
812

20--

PAY TO THE
ORDER OF _____ $ _____

_____ DOLLARS

FOR USE IN CLASSROOM ONLY

FIRST NATIONAL BANK OF DAYTONA BEACH
DAYTONA BEACH, FL 32016

MEMO _____

⑆07820076⑆ 20⑈480056⑈ ⑉108

No. 109

5-94
812

20--

PAY TO THE
ORDER OF _____ $ _____

_____ DOLLARS

FOR USE IN CLASSROOM ONLY

FIRST NATIONAL BANK OF DAYTONA BEACH
DAYTONA BEACH, FL 32016

MEMO _____

⑆07820076⑆ 20⑈480056⑈ ⑉109

DEPOSIT SLIP 1

_____
_____
_____

5-94
812

Date _____ 20 ____

_____

DEPOSIT SLIP

FOR USE IN CLASSROOM ONLY

FIRST NATIONAL BANK OF DAYTONA BEACH
DAYTONA BEACH, FL 32016

:078200762 20:4800056

	DOLLARS	CENTS
CASH		
COINS		
CHECKS–List Singly		
1		
2		
3		
4		
5		
6		
Sub Total		
Less Cash Received		
TOTAL		

_____
_____
_____

5-94
812

Date _____ 20 ____

_____

DEPOSIT SLIP

FOR USE IN CLASSROOM ONLY

FIRST NATIONAL BANK OF DAYTONA BEACH
DAYTONA BEACH, FL 32016

:078200762 20:4800056

	DOLLARS	CENTS
CASH		
COINS		
CHECKS–List Singly		
1		
2		
3		
4		
5		
6		
Sub Total!		
Less Cash Received		
TOTAL		

_____
_____
_____

5-94
812

Date _____ 20 ____

_____

DEPOSIT SLIP

FOR USE IN CLASSROOM ONLY

FIRST NATIONAL BANK OF DAYTONA BEACH
DAYTONA BEACH, FL 32016

:078200762 20:4800056

	DOLLARS	CENTS
CASH		
COINS		
CHECKS–List Singly		
1		
2		
3		
4		
5		
6		
Sub Total		
Less Cash Received		
TOTAL		

DEPOSIT SLIP

_____
_____
_____

5-94
812

Date _____ 20 ___

_____

DEPOSIT SLIP

FOR USE IN CLASSROOM ONLY

FIRST NATIONAL BANK OF DAYTONA BEACH
DAYTONA BEACH, FL 32016

⑈07820076⑉ 2⑈⑉4800056

	DOLLARS	CENTS
CASH		
COINS		
CHECKS–List Singly		
1		
2		
3		
4		
5		
6		
Sub Total		
Less Cash Received		
TOTAL		

_____
_____
_____

5-94
812

Date _____ 20 ___

_____

DEPOSIT SLIP

FOR USE IN CLASSROOM ONLY

FIRST NATIONAL BANK OF DAYTONA BEACH
DAYTONA BEACH, FL 32016

⑈07820076⑉ 2⑈⑉4800056

	DOLLARS	CENTS
CASH		
COINS		
CHECKS–List Singly		
1		
2		
3		
4		
5		
6		
Sub Total		
Less Cash Received		
TOTAL		

_____
_____
_____

5-94
812

Date _____ 20 ___

_____

DEPOSIT SLIP

FOR USE IN CLASSROOM ONLY

FIRST NATIONAL BANK OF DAYTONA BEACH
DAYTONA BEACH, FL 32016

⑈07820076⑉ 2⑈⑉4800056

	DOLLARS	CENTS
CASH		
COINS		
CHECKS–List Singly		
1		
2		
3		
4		
5		
6		
Sub Total		
Less Cash Received		
TOTAL		

CASH RECORD SHEET

Student's Name _____

Date _____

Date	Description	Cash Withdrawals	Payments	Clothing	Entertainment	Food	Housing	Transportation	Miscellaneous

FINANCIAL RECORD SHEET

Student's Name _____

Date _____

Date	Chk.	Description	Receipts	Withdrawals	Payments	Clothing	Entertainment	Food	Health Care	Housing	Transportation	Miscellaneous	Savings/ Investments